Filmguide to

Henry V

C

F 81

INDIANA UNIVERSITY PRESS FILMGUIDE SERIES
Harry M. Geduld and Ronald Gottesman,
General Editors

Filmguide to

Henry V

HARRY M. GEDULD

INDIANA UNIVERSITY PRESS
Bloomington   London

Published in Canada by Fitzhenry & Whiteside Limited, Don Mills, Ontario
Library of Congress Catalog card number: 73-75788
ISBN: 0-253-39313-2 cl.   0-253-29314-6 pa.
Manufactured in the United States of America

For Charlie—who would have done it better—and also for Horst and Evelyn, Ken and Dee, Ken and Betty, Jim and Rita, Murray and Aneta, and Paul and Jean.

contents

preface

As usual, I am indebted to Ron Gottesman and to Carolyn for their unfailing encouragement and invaluable advice. Thanks are also due to Charlie Eckert, Charles Forker, John Gallman, Murdoch Matthew and Murray Sperber for their interest and assistance. Special acknowledgements are due to Marcus—who makes it all worthwhile.

Filmguide to

Henry V

Of all my films I'm fondest of *Henry V* because
in its time it was such an adventure. I saw it
again the other day in Oxford Street. The reaction
of the audience was still absolutely magical.

Laurence Olivier, quoted in *Look,*
January 27, 1970

credits

HENRY V

A Two Cities Film, 1944. Presented by Eagle-Lion.
Released in the U.S.A. by United Artists, 1946.

Producer	Laurence Olivier
Associate Producer	Dallas Bower
Production Supervisor	(For Laurence Olivier Productions)
	Phil Samuels
Director	Laurence Olivier
Assistant Director	Vincent Permane
Screenplay	Laurence Olivier and Reginald Beck
Text Editor	Alan Dent
Film Editor	Reginald Beck
Director of Photography	Robert Krasker
Operating Cameraman	Jack Hildyard
Special Effects	Percy Day
Sound Recorders	John Dennis
	Desmond Dew
Art Director	Paul Sheriff assisted by Carmen Dillon
Costume Designer	Roger Furse assisted by Margaret Furse
Scenic Artist	E. Lindgaard
Continuity	Joan Barry
Make-up	Tony Sforzini
Hairdressing	Vivienne Walker
Chief Electrician	W. Wall
Production Unit	Alec Hayes
	P. G. Bangs
	Laurence Evans
Master of the Horse	John White m. r. c. v. s.

and

The Music of	William Walton

Conducted by Muir Mathieson
Played by The London Symphony Orchestra.
Time: 153 minutes

Filmed from June 9, 1943 to July 12, 1944 at Enniskerry, Eire, and at Denham and Pinewood Studios, England.
World premiere: November 22, 1944 at the Carlton Theatre, London; first shown in the U.S.A., April 6, 1946, in Boston, Massachusetts.
The film is dedicated to the Commandos and Airborne Troops of Great Britain—"the spirit of whose ancestors it has been humbly attempted to recapture. . . ."

CAST
In order of appearance

Chorus	Leslie Banks
Archbishop of Canterbury	Felix Aylmer
Bishop of Ely	Robert Helpmann
The English Herald	Vernon Greeves
Earl of Westmoreland	Gerald Case
Earl of Salisbury	Griffith Jones
Sir Thomas Erpingham	Morland Graham
Duke of Exeter	Nicholas Hannen
Duke of Gloucester	Michael Warre
King Henry V	Laurence Olivier
Montjoy, the French Herald	Ralph Truman
Duke of Berri, French Ambassador	Ernest Thesiger
Corporal Nym	Frederick Cooper
Lieutenant Bardolph	Roy Emerton
Pistol	Robert Newton
Mistress Quickly (The Hostess)	Freda Jackson
Boy	George Cole
Sir John Falstaff	George Robey
King Charles VI of France	Harcourt Williams
Duke of Bourbon	Russell Thorndike
The Constable of France	Leo Genn
Duke of Orleans	Francis Lister
The Dauphin	Max Adrian

The French Messenger	Jonathan Field
Fluellen	Esmond Knight
Gower	Michael Shepley
Jamy	John Laurie
Macmorris	Nial MacGinnis
Governor of Harfleur	Frank Tickle
Princess Katharine	Renee Asherson
Lady Alice	Ivy St. Helier
Queen Isabel of France	Janet Burnell
Court (*Camp-boy*)	Brian Nissen
John Bates	Arthur Hambling
Michael Williams	Jimmy Hanley
A Priest	Ernest Hare
Duke of Burgundy	Valentine Dyall
	and

Infantry and Cavalry by members of the Eirean Home Guard

outline

A playbill fluttering down out of a clear blue sky suddenly fills the screen.* It announces a performance of Shakespeare's Henry V *at the Globe Playhouse on May 1st 1600, and then dissolves into an aerial view of Elizabethan London. The Tower and much of the city north of the Thames is seen in long shot; then, as the camera pulls back (a slow crane-shot) in a south-westerly direction, it reveals old London Bridge and a section of the city on the south bank. It passes the Globe and the "Bear howse," dips momentarily towards the latter, then returns and settles on the theatre. As the camera tilts downwards into the open roof of the Globe, a flag is raised to the top of the theatre's flagpole. A man standing on a platform fastens the flag rope and then sounds two fanfares. The camera now descends into the playhouse, past the orchestra balcony and the audience entering the galleries. Lower still, it shows the groundlings milling about or taking their places before the play begins. As it pans across the motley crowd, we notice an elegantly-dressed gallant wandering among the groundlings, declining fruit offered by an orange-seller, but buying a drink from another vendor. Then, slowly, the camera pulls back and turns to reveal a long-shot view of the auditorium with the apron-stage in the background. Another fanfare is sounded, this time from the orchestra balcony. Then a boy comes from behind the curtains onto the stage and displays a signboard which reads:*

> *The Chronicle History of*
> HENRY THE FIFT
> *with his battel fought at Agin Court*
> *in France*

*This shot is anticipated in another memorable British film, William Cameron Menzies' *Things to Come* (1935) in which it provides a transition from the year 1955 to 1966. H. G. Wells's script for the film describes a "sheet of decaying newspaper . . . fluttering in the wind. It catches on a thorn and as the wind tears at it the audience has time to read. . . ."

As the boy exits, the Chorus enters and receives his applause with a gracious bow. He delivers the play's Prologue, then steps back and pulls aside the stage curtain disclosing a boy with another sign-board on which we read: "Ante chamber in King Henry's Palace". The camera thereupon tilts up to the stage balcony just as the Bishop of Ely and the Archbishop of Canterbury enter from curtains in the rear. They bow to the audience, and act 1 scene 1 of Henry V begins.

Stage balcony. The Archbishop discloses his plan to prevent the passage of a bill that would strip the church of its lands. The clergy will win the sympathies of King Henry by raising a vast sum of money that he can use for his campaign if he decides to go to war with France. In the meantime, the Archbishop has been asked by Henry to find 'legal' justification for his claim to the French throne.

Backstage. The actors are preparing to make their entrances. Here the Elizabethan convention of having boys—in dresses and wigs—play women's roles is briefly but vividly shown.

On stage. Canterbury offers the King elaborate genealogical and documentary evidence to support his claim to the throne of France. The scene is played primarily for laughs. Henry takes his place upon the throne, resolved that "France being ours, we'll bend it to our awe. . . ." The Duke of Berri and a French Herald (Montjoy) appear, bringing a casket of tennis balls: the Dauphin's mocking gift to Henry. The King responds to the insult with great belliger-ence. Rain begins to fall and some of the Globe audience depart as the play continues with a ludicrous quarrel between Pistol and Nym at the Boar's Head tavern. They are interrupted by news that Falstaff is seriously ill. The Chorus now directs our attention to a curtain depicting a stylized view of Southampton which then dis-solves into a scene of Southampton harbor. At this point the film leaves the confines of the Globe and does not return until the final speech of the Chorus.

Southampton. Henry orders the start of his expedition.

The Boar's Head Inn at night. Falstaff, on his deathbed, ap-peals to his "royal Hal." The King's reply (off camera) is the fa-mous rejection speech from 2 *Henry IV* V.v. Outside the Inn, Mistress Quickly describes Falstaff's death to Pistol and his companions, after which the men set out to join the King's campaign.

Now the Chorus asks us to imagine Henry's fleet in mid-Channel. A mist that obscures the Chorus clears momentarily to reveal Henry's ships "on the inconstant billows dancing."

The French court. King Charles VI shows agitation and fear at the news of the English invasion. The Duke of Exeter arrives, bringing Henry's surrender ultimatum to Charles and a message of scorn and defiance to the Dauphin. King Charles collapses in a faint on hearing Henry's threats.

The beach at Harfleur. Henry delivers his speech: "Once more unto the breach. . . ." and cheering English soldiers follow his charge. Fluellen kicks and drives the cowardly Pistol, Nym and Boy into the fray.

Bivouac near Harfleur. A comradely gathering of representatives of the four nations: Fluellen (a Welshman), Gower (an Englishman), Jamy (a Scotsman), and Macmorris (an Irishman) gather during a lull in the siege. For his own amusement, Fluellen foments a quarrel with Macmorris. Gower breaks it up.

Before the gates of Harfleur. Henry stands at the head of his army, outside the city walls, while the Governor delivers up Harfleur to the English.

King Charles's palace. In a terrace garden Princess Katharine receives her first English lesson from the Lady Alice.

Inside the palace. The Dukes of Orleans and Bourbon and the Constable of France gloomily discuss the shameful inaction of the French and the inexplicable "mettle" of the English. Prodded by Queen Isabel, King Charles orders Montjoy, the herald, to take a message of defiance to Henry. The French Dukes are ordered to destroy the English army and capture the English King.

The open countryside. Montjoy confronts Henry who is surrounded by his knights. He tells the English that they are doomed. Henry, in reply, admits that his army is small and enfeebled by sickness, but declares that the English advance will continue.

As the screen darkens, the Chorus (off camera) begins his speech: "Now entertain conjecture of a time. . . ." Gradually, we see the French and English camps at night.

The French camp. Orleans, Bourbon, the Dauphin and the

Constable are waiting impatiently for the day to dawn. They boast about their armor, their horses and the number of Englishmen they expect to kill or capture.

The English camp. Henry, wandering incognito and alone has a brief, comic encounter with the braggart Pistol, observes Fluellen berating Gower for making as much noise as the French, and comes upon three ordinary soldiers, Court, Bates and Williams, seated round a camp fire. Henry joins them and enters upon a discussion of whether the King or his subjects are morally and spiritually accountable for the impending battle. As dawn breaks on the day of Agincourt, Henry, alone by the campfire, utters his soliloquy on ceremony. Sir Thomas Erpingham now appears to tell the King that his nobles, disturbed by his absence, have been seeking through the camp to find him. Commanding that this nobles join him, Henry kneels and prays to the "God of battles" to steel his soldiers' hearts.

The French camp. A blue fleur-de-lys tent flap is swept aside to reveal the French Dukes arming themselves in the bright sunlight, then being escorted to their horses.

The English camp. A group of English nobles are saying a mournful farewell to one another before the battle. Westmoreland's wish that the meager ranks of the English army were supported by "one ten thousand of those men in England/That do not work today" is overheard by Henry and provokes his rousing "Crispin's Day" speech.

Montage of battle preparations in both camps: Henry being helped into his chain mail; the Dauphin being lowered by pulley onto his horse; a line of French drummers; the Dauphin, the Constable and the Dukes of Orleans and Bourbon seated on horseback and drinking triumphant toasts; English soldiers driving in stakes, sharpening them and receiving supplies of arrows.

The English camp. Montjoy appears and offers Henry a last opportunity to ransom himself and surrender his army before his "most assured overthrow." Henry replies defiantly: "Achieve me, and then sell my bones."

The battle of Agincourt. The slow trot of the French cavalry quickens into a charge. The English bowmen await Henry's signal before firing. When it comes, their arrows are released simultaneously, like a dark and deadly cloud which descends upon the

French horsemen and throws them into confusion. A second, advancing wave of French cavalry becomes caught in the wild retreat of the first wave. The English bowmen press forward, firing their arrows as they go. French infantry are trapped, struggling in a swamp. A third wave of French cavalry charges down upon a group of English archers who retreat into a wood. As the French gallop after them, English soldiers drop down from the trees, dragging the French knights off their horses. From a nearby hilltop, the Dauphin, the Constable and Orleans witness the shameful rout of the French army. Vengefully, a group of French knights ride off to the English camp where they kill the camp boys and set fire to the tents. Henry, inflamed by this action which is "expressly against the law of arms," rides into the thick of battle and does single combat with the Constable of France. The fierce duel ends when Henry unhorses his adversary.

End of the battle. Montjoy again appears before Henry, this time humbly to admit the defeat of the French army. The King now receives a tally of the dead. Ten thousand Frenchmen have been slain for an English loss of four nobles and "of all other men but five and twenty score." As the battle episode concludes, the victorious English army, singing 'Non Nobis' and 'Te Deum,' march in winding procession towards the village of Agincourt.

Agincourt village in the snow. Fluellen forces the braggart Pistol to eat a leek as a punishment for mocking the Welsh. Left alone, Pistol resolves to return to England where he will become a cutpurse and claim that the scars he received at Fluellen's hands are actually valorous war wounds.

A hall in the French palace. Henry and his nobles have come together with the French King and his court to discuss terms for ending the war. As mediator, the Duke of Burgundy delivers his great speech on Peace. Henry directs Burgundy to "gain that peace,/With full accord to all our just demands." While the French and English courtiers withdraw to argue the terms of settlement, Henry woos and wins the fair Katharine. King Charles gives his consent to the marriage. Then Henry and Katharine separate, Henry to the left and Katharine to the right. They reappear, robed and crowned, and with their backs to the camera. Joining hands, they proceed to their thrones.

The Globe Theatre. Henry turns and is seen to be wearing the crude make-up in which he first appeared in the Globe Theatre scenes. Then the camera pans to the right and shows a boy made up as Katharine. To the sound of applause, the camera next pulls back, revealing the stage of the Globe Theatre. The Chorus enters and draws a curtain across, concealing the tableau of Henry and Katharine. Walking towards the camera, he throws out his arms and makes the final speech of the play. He concludes, bows, receives the acclaim of a group of Elizabethan gallants. Then the camera tracks upwards, past a stage balcony where the Bishop of Ely is conducting a group of choir boys, past a higher gallery in which the orchestra is playing, up to the platform on which the flagman is pulling down the playhouse flag and rolling it up. Then, out of the Globe to a long shot of Elizabethan London with the Globe Theatre in the foreground. As the camera pulls back to reveal even more of the city, a playbill comes flying down out of the sky and fills the screen. It lists the cast and credits of the film, then dissolves into a final long shot of London in 1600. Momentarily, there is a fade-in to an azure sky; then a fade-out and the film is ended.

the director

Reluctant Filmmaker

Laurence Olivier's heart has always been first and foremost in the theater, not in movies. He was born in Dorking, England, in 1907, the son of a clergyman who encouraged him to take up a theatrical career. Now distinguished as Lord Olivier, he was raised in an atmosphere of genteel poverty which he describes as "probably the most fertile ground for ambition there can be." At school, the young Olivier played Katharine in *The Taming of the Shrew,* and thereafter, in 1925, made his debut in a curtain-raiser at the Brighton Hippodrome. During the twenties his ambition was to become a matinée idol, and he groomed himself to play dashing, romantic roles. Following three seasons with the Birmingham Repertory Theatre (1926–28), he seemed about to realize that ambition: he started to get leads in West End productions. In 1930 he appeared on Broadway in Noel Coward's *Private Lives.* Hollywood beckoned, and soon he had accepted a handsome contract from RKO.

At this period and for some years to come, Olivier regarded film acting simply as a way of earning money quickly. Only theater counted, and so he was not unduly concerned about playing unexceptional roles in undistinguished films. Back in England he returned to the stage, and while alternating with John Gielgud in the roles of Romeo and Mercutio, attracted the attention of director Paul Czinner who offered him the part of Orlando in a film version of *As You Like It* (1936). This, Olivier's first notable film performance, was also his first involvement with a screen adaptation of Shakespeare. He was unimpressed with the results. Czinner's film, together with the Reinhardt-Dieterle film of *A Midsummer Night's Dream* (1935) and Dieterle's film of *Romeo and Juliet* (1936) convinced him at the time that Shakespeare could not be satisfactorily filmed. But subsequently, William Wyler, who directed him as Heathcliff in *Wuthering Heights* (1939), was to change Olivier's mind. However, in the interim, he had returned to the stage, and during two unparalleled seasons at the Old Vic (1937–38) established himself as the century's most versatile and accomplished Shakespearean actor, giving masterly performances as Henry V, Hamlet, Macbeth, Coriolanus, Iago, and Sir Toby Belch. In Hollywood, under Wyler's influence, he overcame his somewhat snobbish disdain for the film medium and began to distinguish himself as a gifted movie actor. His performances as Heathcliff in Wyler's *Wuthering Heights* (1939), as Maxim in Hitchcock's *Rebecca* (1940), as Darcy in Robert Leonard's *Pride and Prejudice* (1940), and as Lord Nelson in Korda's *Lady Hamilton* (1941) provided the measure for all romantic screen portrayals, and the innumerable revivals of these films have testified to their (and to Olivier's) enduring popularity with movie audiences. .

During the Second World War, Olivier served his country in two capacities: as an officer in the Fleet Air Arm and as an actor in such propaganda-oriented feature films as Michael Powell's *49th Parallel* (1941) and Anthony Asquith's *The Demi-Paradise* (1943). *Henry V* (1944), in which he also played the title role, was the first film he directed. Since then, though he has appeared in some fifty screen roles, from Archie Rice in *The Entertainer* (1960) to Mr. Creakle in *David Copperfield* (1970), he has directed only three other films. Two of them were further essays in Shakespeare adaptation (*Hamlet,* 1948 and *Richard III,* 1955) and the third (*The Prince and the Showgirl,* 1958) in which he co-starred with Marilyn Monroe, was an adaptation of a Terence Rattigan play, which David Shipman has not inaccurately described as "a soufflé that failed to rise."

Olivier the actor has been universally praised. He seems physically unexceptional offstage, but he is able, in creating any of his great roles, to use his face, body, and every gesture and movement as entirely controlled, plastic elements of his art. Perhaps his greatest asset is his voice, which, unlike the gentler, poignant vibrato of Gielgud, has a rich, full-bodied power and contributes unforgettably to every line that he delivers.

Olivier's forte has always been the convincing portrayal of triumphant or tragic men of action or power: Coriolanus, Lord Nelson, Henry V, Richard III, John Gabriel Borkman. For an age in which personal heroism has often seemed outmoded or futile,

Olivier has again and again brought heroic characters to life with a rare splendor and fire that justify Sir Cedric Hardwicke's description of him as the last of the great romantic actors.

While few have questioned his stature as an actor, Olivier's achievement as a film director has been frequently challenged. *Henry V* seemingly indicates the limitations of Olivier's interest in the film medium. Some of his critics have argued that he regards the motion picture as just another way of mounting plays, that he is a stylist of adapted works and not a genuine *auteur* who uses the medium to express his own philosophy. Peter Wollen observes that the true *auteur* "does not subordinate himself to another author; his source is only a pretext, which provides catalysts, scenes which fuse with his own preoccupations to produce a radically new work."

Then what of *Henry V*? Is it the film of an *auteur* or a *metteur-en-scènist*? Is it, as Richard Griffith maintained, merely "an antiquarian's version of a national art," a "photographed play"? Or is there, as Andre Bazin insisted, "more cinema, and great cinema at that, in *Henry V* alone than in 90% of original scripts"? It is hoped that the following pages will help the reader to reach his own conclusions about these and other questions concerning this perenially fascinating film.

the production

Origins

The first film version of *Henry V* was not Laurence Olivier's but a silent adaptation made in 1913, featuring the talents of the boys of Shakespeare's school at Stratford-upon-Avon. It is unlikely that Olivier ever saw this primitive effort or that it in any way influenced the making of his own screen version.*

Although, as we have noticed, Olivier's involvements with Shakespeare and the film began in 1936 with his performance as Orlando in Paul Czinner's *As You Like It,* the origins of *Henry V* need be traced back no further than April 1937, when Olivier appeared as King Henry in the Old Vic production directed by Tyrone Guthrie. But the actual idea for a film version of the play must be credited not to Olivier but to Dallas Bower, a sound engineer turned filmmaker, who had been producing and directing films in Britain since 1934. In 1938, Bower prepared a version of *Henry V* for B.B.C. television, but his script was rejected as too ambitious for the new medium. Came the war, and Bower found himself in the army, stationed at Whitby with time on his hands. Picking up his discarded television script, he tried the exercise of turning it into a film scenario. When he was reassigned to the film division of the Ministry of Information, he proposed the production of a film based on his scenario. However, the project made no appeal to his superiors who at that time were interested only in short propaganda and information pictures. By 1942, when Bower left the Ministry to join the B.B.C., nothing had come of his *Henry V* project. It was to be realized only by the coming together of Bower, Olivier, and producer Filippo Del Giudice.

*The following account of Olivier's *Henry V* is heavily indebted for its facts to two books: C. Clayton Hutton's *The Making of Henry V* (London, 1945) and Felix Barker's *The Oliviers* (Philadelphia, 1953). Supplementary details have been drawn from a variety of sources, primarily periodical articles and reviews.

The first stage in this meeting of talents occurred in May 1942 when Bower produced *Into Battle,* a B.B.C. radio program in which Olivier delivered Henry's "Harfleur" and "Crispin's Day" speeches. Olivier had been involved with *Henry V* frequently since 1941 when, with his wife, Vivien Leigh, he had toured air force stations, appearing on behalf of the R.A.F. Benevolent Fund in a concert program that included the wooing scene between Katharine and Henry. And early in 1942, when Olivier was serving in the Fleet Air Arm, he took part in another concert program which included excerpts from *Henry V* with officers, Naval airmen and Wrens [members of the Women's Royal Naval Service] in smaller roles. Accordingly, when Bower raised the idea of a *Henry V* film and mentioned that he had already prepared a screen treatment, Olivier was ready to respond enthusiastically. In part, his response must have been due to Olivier's immediate recognition that a film of *Henry V* could be given topical (propagandist) relevance. However, as neither Bower nor Olivier had financial backing for such a venture, the project was again shelved. The next developments were to occur almost simultaneously in the fall of 1942.

Unexpectedly, Bower found a financial backer for the *Henry V* project. Italian producer Filippo Del Giudice, head of Two Cities Films and one of the unsung heroes of the British film industry, bought Bower's scenario and invited him to join the company. Del Giudice did not share the belief of most British film producers that Shakespeare spelt disaster at the box office; his first concern was not with the project's commercial success or failure but with the problem of who to cast in the role of King Henry. By coincidence, Olivier was then in Manchester rehearsing for a B.B.C. radio production of *Henry V*. Preparations for the film had already begun when Del Giudice tuned in to the radio broadcast of the play. What he heard immediately convinced him that Olivier was the perfect choice for the title role in the film. Bower was promptly assigned the job of contacting Olivier and a meeting was soon arranged in London between the actor and Del Giudice. Olivier's recollections of the encounter have been published in Roger Manvell's *Shakespeare and the Film* (1971): "I think Del heard me doing the 'breach' speech on the radio when I was in uniform, and I first met him, I remember, on the opening night of [the Noel Coward film]

In Which We Serve (1942). I found his attitude in the matter of the obtaining of my services somewhat over-confidently expressed . . . though once I'd started working with him his blazingly flattering convictions of one's worth as an artist were irresistible."

The three persons who were to be most responsible for the film had now come together. Discussion of *Henry V* proceeded while Olivier, under the direction of Anthony Asquith, was creating the role of Ivan Dimitrievitch Kouznetsov in the film, *The Demi-Paradise* (1943; released in the U.S. as *Adventure for Two*). At first, Olivier hesitated about becoming involved in the *Henry V* project. His experiences in British and American film studios had taught him how easily and how frequently good projects were ruined by being assigned to the wrong people. Accordingly, he would agree to take on *Henry V* only if he himself could control all producing and casting decisions. In addition, he insisted that Bower's script be replaced by a new scenario. However, because of Bower's involvement with the project from the very outset, he decided that Bower should be retained as associate producer.

Surprisingly, Del Giudice agreed to Olivier's terms. But now, having got all that he had asked for, Olivier remained uncertain. Was it possible to do a satisfactory screen adaptation of Shakespeare? Who could direct such a picture? He first thought of William Wyler who, as we noticed earlier, had once argued against Olivier's insistence that Shakespeare could not be filmed. By chance the American director was stationed with the American Army Air Force in London. Olivier looked him up and offered him the opportunity to direct *Henry V*. But Wyler was not interested. Though he still asserted that Shakespeare could be filmed, he insisted that he was not the person to do it. Olivier next offered the assignment to Carol Reed and then to Terence Young, but both turned him down. At this point, Olivier decided to direct the picture himself. His many misgivings were offset by Del Guidice's unwavering faith in his abilities. To bolster his confidence further, he appointed Reginald Beck, the editor of *The Demi-Paradise* and a man with wide experience of filmmaking, as his technical adviser. Beck was to collaborate on the new scenario and, ultimately, to be the editor of *Henry V*. He was also to direct many of the scenes in which Olivier himself appeared. William Walton, composer of the score for

Paul Czinner's film of *As You Like It* (in which Olivier had played Orlando) was chosen to write the music for the new Shakespeare film. In casting, Olivier was to select several actors with whom he had already appeared in British films, among them Felix Aylmer (with whom he had acted in *The Demi-Paradise*), Leslie Banks and Robert Newton (in *21 Days* [1940] co-starring Olivier and Vivien Leigh), Nial MacGinnis (in *49th Parallel* [1941] in which Olivier was a French-Canadian trapper), John Laurie and Francis Lister (in *Q Planes* [1939] in which Olivier was a test-pilot).

IN PRODUCTION

Work on the film began in earnest on January 6, 1943. After a busy day on the set of *The Demi-Paradise,* Olivier met with Beck, Bower and some of the technical crew for *Henry V* at Hawksgrove, a house in Fulmer, Buckinghamshire, within easy reach of Denham Studios. Alan Dent, a Shakespeare specialist who was also theater critic for the London *News Chronicle,* had (with Olivier's assistance) already undertaken the editing of the play, and Dent's skillfully edited text became the basis of a new shooting script, prepared in collaboration by Olivier and Beck. In most respects, it was Olivier's inspiration rather than team work that was to determine the quality of the film. As James Agee noticed, "It was Olivier who called in costume designers Roger and Margaret Furse and Roger Ramsdell. . . . It was Olivier who sought out William Walton, whom he regards as 'the most promising composer in England.' It was he who recruited all-important art directors Paul Sheriff and Carmen Dillon. He made use, in fact, of a good deal of talent which most professional moviemakers overlook. And within the profession, he respected professionals more than they usually respect each other. It was chiefly Olivier who did the brilliant casting; he who gave the French court its more-than-Shakespearean character. Many of the most poetic ideas in cutting and transition were also his." However, it was Del Giudice who suggested Robert Krasker as cameraman, despite his lack of experience with Technicolor. The choice of Krasker proved to be masterly, for, as Agee observed, Olivier's cameraman did daring, magnificent new things with color "which Technicolor tradition says must not or cannot be done." One of Krasker's most beautiful shots, filmed at Denham in the early light of dawn, was made "against the shuddering objection of the Technicolor expert." It was the scene before Agincourt, described by Agee as "a crepuscular shot of the doomed and exhausted English as they withdraw along a sunset stream to encamp for the night."

While work was in progress on the shooting script, Dallas Bower had been given responsibility for obtaining the release of certain required actors, artists and technicians from the armed forces. Among them were Roger Furse, Robert Newton and Leo Genn. Olivier himself had already been released from the Fleet Air Arm (a wing of the Navy) to play in *The Demi-Paradise*. Agee commented: "The Royal Navy had given Olivier leave to make *Demi-Paradise* (*Adventure for Two*) in the interest of Anglo-Russian relations, and extended it so that he could make *Henry V* 'in the interest,' says Olivier, 'of Anglo-British relations.'" Bower's assignment was made easier by his influential friends at the Ministry of Information— and perhaps because high-placed government officials could now recognize the propaganda value of such a picture. In due course, Olivier got his actors and technicians over the objections of service chiefs who wanted to retain all available man-power for D-Day. But to his bitter disappointment, he could not secure the services of the actress he wanted for Princess Katharine: his wife, Vivien Leigh. She was still under contract to David Selznick for whom she had played Scarlett O'Hara in *Gone with the Wind*. Selznick refused to release her to play what he regarded as a minor role. Forced to look for another Katharine, Olivier found her in Renee Asherson who was playing in *The Mask of Virtue* at the little Mercury Theatre in Notting Hill Gate, London. In retrospect, it is difficult to imagine any better choice for King Henry's princess than this "substitute casting."

Olivier's solutions to four problems that he considered crucial in adapting *Henry V* to the screen were to give his picture some of its most memorable touches. First and foremost there was the question of how to make Shakespearean language seem natural to the ear of the modern cinema audience. The answer was provided by the solution to an entirely different problem: how to provide a suitable cinematic treatment of Shakespeare's Chorus. Olivier decided that the Chorus would have to look like an Elizabethan actor, and this led him to the idea of opening and closing the film with a performance of the play at the Globe Theatre. This framing device justified his retaining the apology of the Chorus for cramming the "vasty fields of France" within the theatre's "wooden O." But more important, the flamboyant and bombastic prologue in the theatre provided a striking contrast with the more restrained and less "histrionic" blank verse and prose dialogue that followed—thus making most of the film's language seem natural by comparison.

Two other problems led to notable innovations in the film. Olivier was dissatisfied with the traditional method of filming long speeches in Shakespeare (as in George Cukor's *Romeo and Juliet,* 1936) by starting the speech in medium or long shot and gradually moving into an extreme close-up. He had noticed that this technique obliged the actor to lower his voice even though the dramatic intensity of the lines often rose to a climax just before the speech was concluded. Olivier simply reversed the technique—beginning the long speeches in close-up and then pulling back the camera into long shot as the climaxes approached.

Another problem concerned the film's background scenes. Realistic settings would somehow seem inappropriate to the poetic language. But what settings *would* be appropriate? Olivier was later to comment on this question in his program notes on "The Filming of *Henry V.*"

> When the film was first discussed, we decided that the treatment would have to be new, yet in keeping with the period. The middle part of the film especially must have the feeling of the fourteenth century [*sic*], but we would only achieve this aim if the settings and general composition of the shots caught the spirit of fourteenth century paintings. . . . Because the film was planned as a "painter's eye-view" of moving events, we decided to use only painted cut-outs for the background and not solid-built models. This, of course, does not apply to [the model of London at] the beginning of the film. . . .

The specific examples of medieval illustration that Olivier recommended to Paul Sheriff, his art director, were pictures accompanying the text of Froissart and reproductions of calendar pictures by Pol de Limbourg and Jean Colombe in the magnificent manuscript, *Les Très Riches Heures du Duc de Berry,* which was started in 1409 and completed in 1478. The original manuscript of *Les Très Riches Heures,* preserved at the Condé Museum in Chantilly, France, was inaccessible to Olivier and Sheriff in 1943. The reproductions they used were probably the twelve calendar pages published in the art-journal *Verve* 2:7 (April–July 1940). Anyone who has seen the film *Henry V* will probably recall the settings based on medieval illustrations—especially the court of Charles VI, Katharine's castle, and the snow-covered village where Fluellen forces Pistol to eat a leek—as among the most strikingly beautiful scenes in the film. Many who have also seen *Les Très Riches Heures* and medieval illustrations of Froissart have been impressed by the sensitivity and fidelity with which Olivier and Sheriff re-created the spirit of those illuminations and the credibility with which actors appeared against decor that was highly stylized and often deliberately out of perspective.

While Olivier was resolving these general problems, specific tasks were already under way. Color and screen tests for the actors were completed before May 24th when rehearsals began. The battle of Agincourt was the first sequence to be filmed. In its conception, Olivier was inspired by Eisenstein's battle sequence in *Alexander Nevsky* (1938) and also, according to Roger Manvell, by "the massed grouping of horsemen in combat in [Paolo] Uccello's [painting of the] *Rout of San Romano.*"

Under ordinary circumstances, Olivier would have shot his battle sequence in England, using English horsemen and extras. But circumstances were extraordinary. Britain was at war; all available manpower had been drafted into the war effort, and there was no location in England where Olivier could be certain that his filming would not be interrupted by low-flying aircraft. This problem was solved by Dallas Bower who found a suitable location in neutral Eire where adequate manpower was also available. Some of the men recruited in Ireland were "genuine soldiers, being members of the Eirean Home Guard."

On May 24th the film unit crossed the Irish Sea and set up camp on Lord Powerscourt's estate at Enniskerry, near Dublin. In Olivier's words, this camp was run (appropriately) "on strict military lines. Here, under canvas, we had hundreds of players, technical personnel, an armoury, a wardrobe, a mess, workshops and so on." Olivier himself moved into a trailer which became the headquarters of the unit.

There are contradictory reports of the number of men involved. In a June 26 letter, during the shooting of the sequence, Olivier refers to "the whole complement of 664 men." In his program notes that accompanied the release of the picture, he speaks of the problem of costuming "an army seven hundred strong," and mentions "180 horsemen and horses needed for the French cavalry." However, C. Clayton Hutton in his booklet, *The Making of Henry V* (1945) which appears to contain much authoritative information about the film, states that Olivier used 900 horsemen and their horses and 500 foot soldiers. And most recently, Roger Manvell in a note to chapter 4 of his *Shakespeare and the Film* (1971) states that "180 horsemen and 500 footmen of the Eireann Home Guard were employed for the battle scenes."

In order to shoot the charge of the French cavalry, a single-track railroad half a mile long was built alongside a farm road: on it would run the tracking car which carried the camera.

Rehearsals for the Agincourt sequence began on June 1 and almost immediately Olivier ran into a series of accidents, problems and setbacks that were to make this period the most painful, frustrating and costly part of the entire undertaking. Early in the rehearsals he was injured twice: his lip was cut through to the gum when a horse bolted into the camera at the very moment when he was peering through the viewfinder; another time he sprained an ankle and put both arms into slings as a result of over-zealously demonstrating how the English soldiers were to fall from the trees onto the French cavalry.

It was soon discovered that the supply of real armor was inadequate and wartime restrictions on the supply of metal made it impossible to provide sufficient authentic-looking replicas. However, improvized "chain mail" was made out of knitted twine sprayed with aluminum paint. Roger Furse provided many colorful banners which served to conceal improvizations in the armor and also to convey the impression that more men were involved than was actually the case. As Furse managed to turn up a list of the knights who took part in the battle, he was able to research and then recreate for the film the correct coats-of-arms and accoutrements for those who had fought at Agincourt.

The tracking car caused considerable difficulty: it ran forward along the track well enough, but unfortunately it shook from side to side as it moved. Several changes of tires were tried out before the car ran smoothly.

But these were minor matters compared with two serious threats to the continuation of the project: the weather and an unexpected shortage of money. Olivier quickly became aware of the first problem, but for a long time the second remained a private concern of Del Giudice who did not want his director disturbed while the film was being shot. An example of the kind of weather experienced was described by Olivier in a letter to Vivien Leigh: "The sun played lovely games with us all afternoon. Clouds changed their course deliberately from all directions and just got in front of the sun, leaving the sky perfectly blue everywhere else!" Shooting began on June 9 and continued through July 22: a total of thirty-nine days to shoot a sequence that was to have a screen time of a little less than seventeen minutes. On fourteen of those thirty-nine days, heavy rain made shooting impossible; on several other days the sky was too overcast to permit more than an hour or two of filming.

Black-and-white rushes were shown to Olivier every second day while he was in Eire, and he noticed technical defects in this footage that required some four-and-a-half minutes (screen time) of retakes. The rushes depressed him as much as the weather because he was not used to the inferior quality of black-and-white prints struck from Technicolor film.

While the rains poured down in Ireland, Del Giudice in London was weathering a financial crisis that threatened the completion of the film. The Agincourt sequence alone had already cost about £80,000 ($320,000) out of a projected budget of £300,000 ($1,200,000) for the whole picture. Suddenly, the film's major investor withdrew his financial backing and Del Giudice found himself in desperate need of someone who could put up the rest of the money. A backer was found in the person of movie magnate J. Arthur Rank, who agreed to underwrite the film on two conditions: that *Henry V* would cost no more than the projected £300,000, and that Del Giudice's company become a subsidiary of the Rank Organization. Reluctantly, Del Giudice bowed to his terms, and *Henry V* was saved. But before the film was completed, expenses were to soar far above the agreed ceiling. The final cost of *Henry V* was to be £475,708 (approximately two million dollars)—and the independence of Two Cities Films.

Meanwhile, Olivier, having finished work on location in Eire, returned to England to shoot the rest of the picture. There were serious problems here too, as Olivier himself subsequently recalled: "Conditions . . . were very far from favorable. We had only one Technicolor camera in the country, no quick cranking gear box, equipment at Denham so incomplete that an entirely new and costly lamp-hanging job had to be done if one wished to turn the camera from one to the opposite direction. Days and days of precious time were wasted owing to this and other disadvantages naturally imposed by wartime conditions." (Roger Manvell, *Shakespeare and the Film* (1971), quoting material received from Olivier).

The filming proceeded in spite of the difficulties. Just over a week was taken up with tests of the artistes and make-up. Then, on August 9 Olivier began shooting scenes in the Denham film studios. The studio filming continued for 112 days, and another twelve days were occupied with work on the lot. This section of *Henry V*, completed by January 3, 1944, was to provide just over 153 minutes of the film in its final form.

The next two months, January 5 through March 11, were taken up with filming models, inserts and special effects. In his program notes to the film Olivier observed:

> While on the subject of models, we felt we achieved a minor triumph in dealing with the model shot of the invading English fleet. The Technicolor camera, unlike the black and white film camera, has no variable speeds and, therefore, we were denied the normal means of getting the effect of perfect natural movement in the model ships. We could perform no camera tricks, but with considerable ingenuity eventually succeeded in getting the ships to move at the correct roll and speed for the Technicolor camera.

The most memorable model shots, those of Elizabethan London with which the film was to open and conclude, had to be filmed separately during April 22 through May 10 because the giant model of London was not ready until mid-April. This model, based on J. C. Visscher's early seventeenth century map-view of the city, was fashioned in wood and plaster and measured fifty by seventy feet. North of the Thames it showed Elizabethan London from Ludgate Hill to the Tower and included the Guildhall, old St. Paul's, numerous city churches, and old London Bridge. To the south, across the river, could be seen the Bankside, the Bear Garden, the Globe Theatre, and the church of St. Mary Overbury (now known as Southwark Cathedral). According to an anonymous columnist in the *New York Herald-Tribune* (April 14, 1946) the model took more than a year to construct. However, Olivier states in his program notes that it took only two or three months to make. He adds that it was built "in the pattern shop at Denham, was housed in two large tents, and then grouped piece by piece round the big tank at the studios."

Much technical work remained to be done on the film. William Walton's music and the sound effects for the film had been recorded during the latter half of March and early April. Composing and synchronizing the music, especially for the battle sequence, had, in Walton's own words, involved "an unusually complex and close collaboration of sound and screen from one bar or visual movement to the next," a procedure evidently modeled on the montage of music and visuals that Prokofiev and Eisenstein had attempted in *Alexander Nevsky* (1938). The task of combining the music, dialogue and sound effects with edited film footage extended over two months from May 11 through July 12, when the film was sent back to the laboratory for final processing. Felix Barker notes that Olivier was still doubtful and depressed with his work "until the day when the rough-cut was synchronized with the score which William Walton had composed"; it was only then that he realized "that even if it was a financial failure, people could not say it was bad."

Although *Henry V* was the first film Olivier had directed and he had overshot the budget agreed upon by Rank and Del Giudice, there had been little or no wastage or unnecessary expense in the production. Thus Olivier's cutting ratio (the amount of wasted footage compared to film actually used in the final print) was only about 1.25:1—whereas in Hollywood at that time a ratio of 15:1 was considered economical.

Mainly on account of wartime conditions it had taken thirteen months to shoot and process the picture. Another four months were to elapse before preparations were ready for the premiere of *Henry V*.

The film opened on November 22, 1944 at the Carlton Theatre, London. The reviewers were generally enthusiastic and the film even earned the unique distinction of becoming the subject of a leading article in the London *Times*. But public interest in the picture was at first only lukewarm. Then, mainly through word-of-mouth recommendations, the response suddenly quickened: long lines formed outside the theatre. The run at the Carlton was extended from one month to three, then the film was transferred to the Marble Arch Pavilion where it ran for another eight months before going on general release.

The American premiere of *Henry V* was delayed until April 6, 1946, when the film was presented in Boston under the auspices of the Theater Guild. The New York opening followed on June 17, at the City Center, 131 West 55th Street, before an audience that included Olivier and Vivien Leigh, a large number of U.N. delegates, and a spectrum of celebrities from the worlds of theater, film, society and business. In New York City the film ran for almost a year. Film industry executives on both sides of the Atlantic had expressed grave doubts about the box office potential of *Henry V*. Past experiences had convinced them that there was no profit to be made from movie versions of Shakespeare. But such misgivings were proved groundless as *Henry V* went from city to city drawing packed audiences and racking up healthy returns. Though it was not to become a box office "blockbuster" on the scale of *Gone With the Wind,* its financial success encouraged the production of other Shakespeare films, including Olivier's versions of *Hamlet* and *Richard III*. The critical success of *Henry V* has never been in doubt since the British premiere, when such critics as Edgar Anstey and C. A. Lejeune hailed the picture as "a memorable event" and "a salute to high adventure," and since the American premiere when James Agee admitted that he could not think of any film that "seems to be more beautiful, more skilfully and charmingly achieved within its wisely ordered limits, or more satisfying." Olivier's film brought him a special Oscar, the New York Critics' award (Best Actor), and the National Board of Review award (Best Actor). Other, international prizes and honors showered on the film are too numerous to mention here. Olivier himself, reflecting recently on *Henry V,* called it "a rather sweet film. I like it," he said. "I feel proud of it."

analysis

Critical discussion of *Henry V* has tended to focus on the same questions. Is Olivier's film faithful to the letter and spirit of Shakespeare's play? If not, how and why did Olivier depart from his source? Are the various visual styles relevant? Are they integrated? How appropriate and effective are Olivier's structural and cinematic devices (such as the Globe Theatre frame and the transition from the playhouse to Southampton)? How satisfactory was Olivier's casting and Walton's music? Does *Henry V* work successfully as film art on the one hand and as a topical propaganda picture on the other? Are there any conflicts between these objectives? Finally, aside from the film's topical relevance in 1944 and its being an adaptation of Shakespeare, to what extent does it embody or express any personal statement by Olivier himself? Most of these questions will be considered in the commentary that follows.

The reader is warned not to expect an analysis of Shakespeare's play. Our emphasis here is on the film and not on its literary source, though the relationship of the movie and the drama on which it is based must be considered, of course. It is, however, assumed that any reader seriously interested in Olivier's film will already have familiarized himself with the play. Consequently, discussion of Shakespeare's plot, themes and characterization will be minimal and lengthy quotations or summary of passages in the play will be avoided.

The film will be considered in four sections (1) the introductory Globe Theatre scenes; (2) scenes following the transition out of the Globe but preceding the battle; (3) the battle of Agincourt; (4) all the scenes following the battle. These are the *film's* natural, structural divisions; they do not invariably relate to the content or to the act and scene arrangement of the original play.

1. *The Introductory Scenes*

Aside from establishing much of the introductory material from Shakespeare's play (characters, themes, situations, etc.) the opening scenes of Olivier's *Henry V* have several important functions. First they introduce a pattern of frameworks for the film's action. These frameworks are essentially shows arranged one inside the other like Chinese boxes. The outermost show is the apparently realistic view of Elizabethan London revealed to us by the filmmaker. Within this show is the theatrical show presented to us by the Chorus who, in due course directs us to the third and most spectacular show: the battle of Agincourt "directed" by King Henry V. Secondly, the Globe scenes begin with two indications that music will have an important role in what follows: the flagman opens the theatre and introduces the show by sounding two fanfares; then, a moment later, even before we see the Globe audience or the stage, the orchestra comes into view, striking up an overture to the play. Third, Olivier paradoxically uses the theatre scenes to expose the limitations of theatre, in preparation for the break away from the theatre's confines. While he goes to considerable pains to show us what an original production at the Globe might have been like, he actually presents these scenes with the freedom of the camera rather than the restricted viewpoint of a theatre spectator. Thus, we first see the Chorus in an establishing long shot from high angle position (view from the gallery), then in close shot at eye-level (an ideal view from the main floor of the theatre), then in close-up (an exclusively cinematic viewpoint), then, gradually, in long shot at eye level as the camera slowly pulls back during his speech. Collectively these viewpoints are impossible to a single spectator in the playhouse; in effect we are being told that the techniques of cinema can show us a play more effectively than we could ever see it in an actual theatre. The gaffes of the performance, the inadequate conventions, the Chorus's direct appeals to the imagination of the audience, and our constant awareness of the boisterous groundlings also underline the shortcomings of theatre as a medium for presenting a dramatic epic like *Henry V*. Olivier cleverly obscures the unnaturalness (to the film audience) of blank verse dialogue by diverting our attention from Shakespeare's language to a contrast between the "real" Globe audience and the histrionics they are enjoying. James Agee objected to the "subtly patronizing way" in which the opening Globe sequence was done. "We have a right," he observes, "to assume that the Elizabethan stage at its best was in its own terms as good as the theater or the screen can ever hope to be, and I wish this might have been suggested—as it is in flashes by Olivier—without even the faintest suggestion of *Murder in the Red Barn,* or of 'life ran very high in those days.'" Agee's objection seems, however, to miss the point. The "subtly patronizing" manner is a deliberate "put-down" of theatre in favor of film as a medium for the kind of dramatic work that is being presented. Olivier wants us to believe, temporarily, the opposite of what we normally assume: that the theatre cannot effectively create or sustain dramatic illusion, while film is the perfect medium for fantasy and unreality, the place where the language of poetic drama naturally belongs. Thus, paradoxically but also quite deliberately, he makes the theatre scenes appear more realistic than many of the later scenes in which there are no histrionics and no distractions from the blank verse.

Shakespeare purists have found much to complain about in the Globe scenes. Students of the Elizabethan theatre can point to errors and improbabilities in the reconstruction of the mise-en-scène, while critics interested in Olivier's adaptation of the play can, justifiably, object to his distortion of I.i and I.ii by turning much of it into comedy. The Bishop of Ely (Robert Helpmann) has been transformed into a ludicrous and rather naive figure, mocked by and embarrassed at the catcalls of the groundlings, who stupidly expresses his childish fit of pique at the Archbishop by tossing a sheaf of documents into the air. The Archbishop (Felix Aylmer), made to look ridiculous simply by his walking on stage with mitre askew, has been reduced to a stuffy, pedantic, schoolmasterly type who lectures both Henry and the Globe audience. The distortion of I.i and I.ii for comic effect serves, intentionally, to obscure the actual words of the two prelates. Olivier does not want us to become too aware of the duplicities and complex motivations behind the "justifications" that the Archbishop offers for Henry's invasion of France. (Raymond Durgnat has reasonably objected to this scene on the grounds that it gives moral license to jingoism.) In addition, Olivier does not wish to bore us with a deadly serious presentation of the Archbishop's long and important but dramatically very dull speech on the Salic Law. So the prelates become amusing characters and the long speech is almost lost amid the buffoonery over the documents. And so too Olivier actually leaves in the specious justification for Henry's invasion, but plays the scene so that we hardly notice its speciousness amid the comedy. By the time the French ambassador arrives, somehow or other Henry's forthcoming campaign seems to have been "justified" without our noticing precisely how.

In contrast, the supercilious manner of the French ambassador (The Duke of Berri, played by Ernest Thesiger) and the Dauphin's insolent gift to Henry immediately establish the French as an arrogant people who need to be put in their place. Henry at first reacts to the gift with a good-humored smile (he can take a joke against himself), but the smile promptly gives way to a different mood: a fiery outburst in which he threatens dire consequences for a joke that is also an insult to the State he represents. It is the first rousing speech in the film and it instantly affirms Henry's strength of character: he is a man of action and authority with whom it is a disastrous mistake to trifle. The King, having given short shrift to the French ambassador, now demonstrates his brisk resolution by ordering immediate preparations for war with France. And when he makes his exit he leaves neither the Globe audience nor the movie audience in any doubt that he is the man in command of the situation.

The Chorus (Leslie Banks) now enters and draws a curtain across the inner stage. In so doing he reveals, depicted on the curtain, a stylized view that will form part of the background to the first comedy scene. Almost imperceptibly the movie audience is being prepared for another scene that will soon follow, when the Chorus will draw across the inner stage another curtain whose stylized view of Southampton harbor becomes the transition out of the Globe. At this point, however, our attention is caught less by the convention of the curtain-scenery than by the excited flourishes, the passionate, enthusiastic words of the Chorus as he takes up the spirit of chivalry and jingoism:

"Now all the youth of England are on fire. . . ."

At the conclusion of his speech, he exits and two stage hands appear carrying bundles of hay. There is a peal of thunder and they look upwards. In a low angle shot through the open roof of the Globe we glimpse a dark cloud covering the sun. Then, in a high angle shot we see rain suddenly pouring down on the theatre audience. The less hardy members depart. Meanwhile, on a balcony above the stage a boy appears with a placard for the Boar's Head inn, which he displays to the audience, then suspends like a regular inn sign out over the stage. As the camera tracks in towards the balcony, Nym makes his appearance. He pokes his head through the balcony curtains and begins to climb down to the apron stage. In close-up he drops beside Bardolph who is standing up and watching him good-humoredly. The low comedy characters in the scene that follows are shot almost entirely from low angle positions —that is, from the viewpoint of the groundlings. In so doing, Olivier reverses the usual practice of employing low angle shots to emphasize or suggest the power or importance of characters. (All other scenes in the Globe are shot either from eye level or high angle positions.) Curiously, while Olivier uses the freedom of the movie camera to show us the Globe theatre production, he also employs, just for the comedy scene, camera angles that are more typical of theatre viewpoints (and perhaps indicative of class divisions within the theatre audience) than of film technique.

Pistol (Robert Newton) enters accompanied by the Hostess (Mistress Quickly, played by Freda Jackson). Robert Newton's performance belongs less to Shakespeare than to the actor's own memorable gallery of film grotesques (Lukey in *Odd Man Out,* Mr. Brodie in *Hatter's Castle,* and Long John Silver in *Treasure Island*). The swagger and braggadocio of this *miles gloriosus* parody the chivalrous spirit of Henry and his court and the jingoistic speech of the Chorus. He exemplifies the identification of English cowardice exclusively with the comic figures. Pistol is promptly established as the most entertaining and important of the comic characters. Only Pistol is greeted with wild delight by the groundlings; only Pistol communicates intimately with the audience, mocking the other comic characters in his asides. The groundlings seem to be responding to a star comedian rather than to the role he is playing. Certainly they react to him before he has begun his scene with Nym and Bardolph. James Agee rather harshly objected to the performance of Freda Jackson (Mistress Quickly) as "the only embarrassing bit of amateurishness" in the film, though he admits that she "gave her lines much tenderness and thought" in delivering her speech on Falstaff's death. More objectionable, perhaps, are the performances of Nym (Frederick Cooper) and Bardolph (Roy

Emerton). Both reduce the characters they are playing to types of slapstick comedy or pantomime. Cooper's Nym becomes the superficial stock figure of the belligerent, ill-tempered little man (the type that Oliver Hardy confronted on innumerable occasions). Roy Emerton's Bardolph is a stuttering oaf, somewhat reminiscent of Lennie in the film version of Steinbeck's *Of Mice and Men*. Both interpretations seem irrelevant to the nature of the adaptation. However, it is arguable that this is part of Olivier's intentional setting up of the audience (of the film) to accept the more natural playing that is to follow.

Regrettably, the film dilutes the original comedy of Pistol's quarrel with Nym. There are too many distractions from the situation: Pistol's grotesqueness and the slapstick style of the other two comic figures, the Hostess's hysterical giggle at her own bawdy jokes, Pistol communing with the groundlings, their reactions to him, and our awareness of the Globe audience laughing at lines that are less than immediately comprehensible (let alone amusing) to us. When, at the end of the scene, the three characters take their bow, we are left with the impression that the comedy material has been directed more exclusively than any previous scenes to one specific section of the Globe audience, and that the performances of the comedians are more self-conscious, more in the nature of theatrical "turns" than any of the other acting we have seen so far.

2. *Out of the Globe*

After the comic characters have made their exit, the Chorus draws another curtain across the inner stage. Depicted on it is a stylized view of Southampton harbor. The Chorus directs the audience's attention to it while asking them to linger their patience on:

> . . . we'll digest
> The abuse of distance; force a play;
> The king is set from London, and the scene
> Is now transported, gentles, to Southampton.
> There is the playhouse now, there must you sit,
> And thence to France. . . .

The camera, no longer confined within the theatre's wooden O, tracks towards the curtain. The Chorus goes out of view as the curtain's stylized scene comes into close-up; then the stylized scene dissolves into a medium long-shot of Southampton harbor—at first looking exactly as it appeared on the curtain. As the camera tilts downwards, we see from high angle the stern of a ship moored at the quayside. Henry and his knights are receiving benediction from the Archbishop of Canterbury. The scene now looks like a three-dimensional stage setting (ship) with a flat, painted and stylized background depicting a castle tower. That is, the movement out of the Globe focuses first on a scene that combines in its setting both stylization and theatrical realism. Next, Henry is seen in close-up, donning a magnificent white hat. (Momentarily, Olivier here reproduces a traditional portrait of Henry V and thus moves, briefly, into formal pictorialization.) Then, promptly, he shifts to the quasi-naturalistic: the camera follows Henry as he steps ashore (away from the theatrical "ship") and walks along the quay. Stamping his seal on a document, he declares

> Cheerly to sea, the signs of war advance;
> No King of England, if not King of France.

With Henry's couplet the music mounts to a crescendo, and the scene dissolves as the first English cannon is being hoisted aboard ship. Thus upon taking us out of the theatre, Olivier introduces us in one short scene, to the various visual styles that will become familiar in the rest of the film.

So far, however, little has been made of the camera's mobility in contrast to the restrictive viewpoints of the theatre scenes. The Southampton scene still seemed largely theatrical, even though it had been arrived at by a cinematographic trick. With the next scene, however, we become more conscious of the camera's freedom than at any time since the opening shots of the film. The music's crescendo dies away as the quayside preparations dissolve into a shot of the Boar's Head tavern at night. A light is visible in an upper, open window. The camera pulls back, then tracks forward and moves up to and in through the window. The voice-over words of the Chorus (now unseen) remind us how far we have come from the theatre's limitations:

> . . . still be kind
> And eke out our performance with your mind.

Inside the inn, the camera comes to rest on what looks momentarily like a Dutch or Flemish interior painting by Pieter de Hooch or Van Eyck. Mistress Quickly, wearing a wide-brimmed straw hat, is bending over Falstaff (George Robey), as he lies inert on his deathbed. The stillness, delicate lighting and careful composition of the scene contrast strikingly with the free movement into it from the dark and almost formless exterior of the inn. The Hostess goes out of the bedchamber and Falstaff, haggard and distraught, sits up and addresses "royal Hal," his former partner-in-rascality. Then, off camera, the voice of Henry can be heard rejecting Falstaff:

I know thee not, old man, fall to thy prayers. . . .

Falstaff collapses onto his pillow and fumbles with the sheets. Now the Hostess re-enters and sits beside the bed on which Falstaff lies dead.

Olivier's addition of this death scene can be justified first as an unequivocal reminder that Henry has renounced his former waywardness, and secondly as an indication that corruption in the attractive guise of frivolous irresponsibility has been exorcised from the kingdom. The English have serious affairs to settle, and Falstaff's rascality is a distraction that must be removed before the campaign begins. It is less easy to justify George Robey's characterization of Falstaff. Nothing about his performance tells us that the character was once the most engaging of all knaves, the supreme self-indulgent braggart. Perhaps Olivier expected something of Falstaff's former character to be suggested by George Robey's reputation as a stage comedian: he was the self-styled "Prime Minister of Mirth." But, unfortunately, Robey's stage reputation does not serve his performance in *Henry V,* in which he conveys little more than the impression of a horror-stricken, hollow-eyed old man being cruelly spurned in his hour of greatest need.

The death scene dissolves to the outside of the Boar's Head at dusk. Nym, the Boy, Bardolph, Pistol and the Hostess leave the inn and gather pensively around a cart in the inn yard. The scene that now unfolds is brief, static and somewhat theatrical, but it is played with tenderness and evokes a memorable mood picture in which pathos, compassion, the sense of loss and the bitter-sweet moment of parting combine to move us profoundly and ineffably. The scene opens with the characters viewed in medium shot, but as the Hostess recounts the passing of Falstaff, the camera tracks in to a close-up of her face. The close-up is held until the speech is almost at an end; whereupon the camera tracks slowly back to take in the reactions of the whole group in medium shot. Here the camera movement is almost imperceptible, but it is the same movement that will be used more strikingly later in the film, for those scenes in which Henry delivers his impassioned speeches at Harfleur and on St. Crispin's Day.

Shakespeareans may, reasonably, object to Freda Jackson's rendering of the Hostess's speech. Her deeply emotional delivery somewhat obscures the ironies in that immortal description of Falstaff's last moments. Nevertheless, the speech comes across with a feeling that is consistent with the poignancy into which the whole scene develops and which is underscored by Walton's music, by the glimpse of the Hostess tenderly kissing the Boy's brow, and by Pistol's mock heroic-pathetic farewell as he marches off into the night and away to the wars.

The music dies away and we begin to hear the voice of the Chorus. Out of a dark screen the Chorus is slowly faded in until he appears—removed from the Globe setting—in close-up against a formless mauve background. As he describes the embarkation of the English fleet and invites us to behold "A city on the inconstant billows dancing," the camera tracks back until he can be seen in long shot, addressing us out of the void. Then a mist starts to obscure him. In a few moments he is lost to sight. Now, through the mist, we catch a glimpse of the English fleet; then the scene is again obscured. Above the mist we next see, momentarily, a long-shot view of the French palace, and this view then dissolves into a high angle shot of the palace interior.

This transition, which shifts the action from England to France, is a choppy, incoherent sequence. Since the camera has already broken out of the confines of the Globe, there seems no justification for showing us the Chorus again. His emergence, evidently out of the void, dissociates him not only from the Globe setting but also from the scenes that precede and follow his reappearance. His words, describing the "huge vessels through the furrow'd sea . . . / Breasting the lofty surge," are instantly belied by the shot of a few tiny stylized and almost toy-like ships representing the English fleet. However, despite the awkwardness of the sequence, it does prepare us to some extent for the highly stylized interior of the palace. In a few shots, Olivier moves from actors in an illusionistic setting (outside the Boar's Head), to an "actor" removed from all settings (Chorus), to stylized scenes *without* actors (shots of the fleet and the palace exterior), and thence to a stylized scene *with* actors.

Now it is as if the figures in a medieval illuminated manuscript had suddenly quickened into life. At first the characters in the French court are seen motionless, apparently mere elements of the setting. Then they begin to move as if in separate panels of a large picture, exhibiting variously attitudes of indolence, lethargy, indifference or nervousness in response to the news that the English have begun their invasion. The Duke of Orleans (Francis Lister) plays idly with a cup and ball; the Constable of France (Leo Genn) stands in a formal pose, appearing more bored than chivalrous despite his resplendent armor; the Dauphin (Max Adrian), looking even more bored, gazes out of a window; the Duke of Berri scrutinizes an illuminated manuscript—presumably *Les Très Riches Heures*—while King Charles (Harcourt Williams) seated in a most undignified manner at the base of a pillar, stares nervously about him.

Throughout this scene, Olivier endeavors to reduce incongruities between the stylized two-dimensional set and his three-dimensional actors. He achieves his objective to some extent by lighting and color coordination of costumes and setting. But his main method is to keep the scene relatively static so that the actors always seem to belong to the pictorial composition. Camera movement is negligible and characters tend to move from one formal pictorial arrangement into another. The result is closer to a succession of separate, beautifully composed pictures than a single coherent dramatic scene. The first considerable camera movement occurs, appropriately, with the arrival of the Duke of Exeter (Nicholas Hannen), rousing the French with Henry's demand that King Charles promptly surrender his throne. But this movement quickly settles on a formal composition—like a medieval tapestry—in long shot, depicting Charles and his court receiving Henry's emissary. This same tendency for characters to be disclosed in or move into stylized pictorial arrangements is also evident in the use of close-ups and two-shots. A notable example occurs near the end of the scene where Exeter confronts the Dauphin with Henry's message of scorn and defiance. The two men move out of close-ups in which they are seen against the elaborate set into a two-shot in which the Dauphin (clad in blue) stands on one side of a pillar, and the Duke of Exeter (clad in red) stands on the other side: together they create separate panels of a colorful, ornamental diptych.

This palace scene provides our first general impression of the French—and it is not a favorable one. They appear to range between two extremes represented by the brazen arrogance of the Dauphin and the timorousness and lack of authority displayed by the king. The interpretations of these extreme roles present interesting contrasts. Harcourt Williams' King Charles is virtually a caricature of the Shakespearean original. The monarch who, in the play, is prudent but far from irresolute, who declares: "Think we King Harry strong;/ And princes, look you strongly arm to meet him," is transformed in the film into a dithering dotard who faints at a mere threat from the English. Later scenes also convey the impression that he is henpecked by his somewhat shrewish queen, Isabel. On the other hand, Max Adrian suggests a few interesting aspects of the Dauphin's character that are not discernible in the play but nevertheless enrich the role and make it particularly memorable. To the brash overconfidence which characterizes the Dauphin in the text, Adrian (and Olivier) add some plausible insights into the relationship of the Dauphin and his father. We see the prince smirk at the king's faint-heartedness and flaunt his own arrogant underestimate of Henry before Charles's displays of fear and weakness. We also see the king, in a subsequent scene, fussing over the Dauphin and, to the prince's obvious embarrassment, treating him like a small boy who has to be put in his place. Later, we are shown the Dauphin's cowardice. Before Agincourt he boasts about the number of English prisoners he will capture, but during the actual fighting he remains in safety, upon a distant hill, from which he watches the destruction of the French army. Max Adrian's Dauphin is the spoiled son of a weak father: a vain, supercilious braggart who scorns in others the cowardice he displays himself.

The fears that storm through the French king's mind give way to a glimpse of the stormy waters of the English Channel, and the ornamentations and artificialities of the French court give way to the realities of the English invasion. As Charles faints away before the Duke of Exeter, the scene dissolves into a shot of wild, surging waves. Then in a brief montage we see English soldiers pouring onto the beach at Harfleur and dragging a cannon ashore. The voice-over commentary of the Chorus simultaneously invites the audience to

> Work, work your thoughts . . . [and]
> Behold the ordnance on their carriages. . . .

This commentary works as subtle flattery of the audience, suggesting that *we* are actually creating all these splendid images in our heads.

Now the English troops can be seen, in long shot, retreating through a breach in the cliffs. As the camera begins to track forward, Henry appears, on horseback. He removes his helmet, rides up to his men and begins his speech: "Once more unto the breach. . . ." The camera focuses on Henry in close-up; then, as his speech continues, it slowly cranes upwards until—as he comes to the climax of his speech—we see Henry in high angle, long shot from a position above the crow's nest of one of his invasion vessels. Henry's undoubted leadership and resolution contrast sharply with the incapacity of the French king, but the effect of looking down upon him while he is delivering his stirring lines is to suggest that, despite his obvious valor, he has begun his campaign as the underdog.

Aroused by Henry's words, the cheering English troops follow their king's charge into the breach. Now comes a moment of slapstick in which English cowardice—again associated only with the comic characters—is mocked and counteracted. Pistol and his companions try to hold back, cowering beneath a rock, but Fluellen (Esmond Knight) spies them and drives them into the action, using the flat of his sword against Pistol's rump. It is the first of two scenes in which Pistol is humiliated by Fluellen, and the last scene in which the other comic characters appear.

Shots of a cannon breaching a wall precede the interlude of the four captains. Fluellen's "joshing" of the Irish captain, Macmorris

(Nial MacGinnis), an episode removed in spirit and substance from the more serious main action, is not inappropriately played against a painted landscape. (In later scenes the English troops are generally seen against backgrounds of real countryside.) The ferocity shown by Fluellen in his handling of Pistol is somewhat mitigated in the four captains scene by his display of a rather mischievous sense of humor. However, the close-ups of Esmond Knight rather disconcertingly emphasize his glass eye (Knight was blinded in action during the Second World War) and make him appear almost as grotesque as Robert Newton's Pistol. John Laurie's performance as Jamy, the Scottish captain, is an accomplished vignette, but Nial MacGinnis is weakly cast as a rather wooden, doltish Macmorris, and Michael Shepley's Gower, the English captain, suffers from being overly reminiscent of Colonel Blimp or Nigel Bruce's Dr. Watson. The scene is largely theatrical, but at least one effective use of film is notable in the quarrel of Fluellen and Macmorris when the latter's mounting anger is shown by the movement of his head slowly up into the frame.

At the sound of a trumpet, the four captains grab their helmets and head for the walls of Harfleur. There is a dissolve into a long shot showing Henry at the head of his army, addressing the Governor of Harfleur (Frank Tickle) who stands on the battlements above the gates of his city. The scene contrasts the English in their "real" armor with the French inside their "artificial" city. As in many medieval illustrations, the height of the walls seems proportionally too small for the figures who appear on them. The camera tracks in to a close-up in which the Governor, flanked by two men who look like executioners, proclaims the surrender of Harfleur. Again we see Henry diminished from high angle position (the Governor's viewpoint) as he tells his brother, the Duke of Gloucester (Michael Warre), to enter the city, fortify it against the French, and treat the surrendered garrison with mercy. While the English troops enter the gates of Harfleur, Henry walks to the right of the screen and gazes curiously across the landscape of the country he has come to conquer.

A dissolve takes us, appropriately, to our first sight of Henry's ultimate conquest: the Princess Katharine (Renee Asherson). A long shot of the exterior of the French palace is followed by a view of the garden terrace overlooking the battlements. The terrace door opens and the Lady Alice (Ivy St. Helier) enters followed by the Princess. In the courtyard below, Montjoy (Ralph Truman) is about to escort Exeter on the start of his journey back to the English army. As they wait for the gates to be opened, the men glance up at the terrace and pay their acknowledgements to the Princess. Katharine proceeds into the garden and, while she is cutting flowers, receives her first English lesson from the Lady Alice. This is a scene of great charm. Even audiences who can understand very little of the French dialogue are unlikely to remain insensitive to the subtle mixture of deference, flattery and whimsy with which Ivy St. Helier's Alice tutors her Princess; while Renee Asherson's Katharine seems in face, form and manner to have stepped out of the pages of *Les Très Riches Heures*. She is a story-book princess cutting story-book flowers in a story-book palace. And when her lesson has ended, with perfect elegance appropriate to a lady of the age of chivalry, she catches up her skirts before her and leads Alice in majestic procession out of the garden.

From a balcony, Katharine observes that Montjoy has returned, while on the horizon she can see Essex and his party riding away. Followed by Alice, she descends a staircase into the banqueting hall where she and her lady-in-waiting take their places at the royal dining table. In yet another picture-book setting, the French once again display their indecision and lethargy. Only the Constable of France reveals himself to be a man of spirit, urging the king to immediate action against the enemy. But his speech merely inspires the Duke of Orleans to philosophize on the "mettle" of the English, while the Duke of Bourbon utters strong words that succeed only in shocking Queen Isabel. The Queen thereupon prods the king who wakes up, and in an unimpressive show of command, orders Montjoy to take a message of defiance to Henry, and the three Dukes—Orleans, Bourbon and the Constable—to capture Henry and bring him to Rouen. Much against his will, the Dauphin is ordered to remain at court; to pacify his would-be valiant offspring, Charles kisses him and pats his face, to the prince's obvious discomfiture.

Next, in long shot we see Montjoy, accompanied by heralds and a standard-bearer, riding through the fields of Picardy to deliver his king's message. In the open countryside, Montjoy, clad in the

elegant costume of the court and seated comfortably and command-
ingly on horseback, is received by a weary King Henry, clad in
armor and standing humbly on foot. Montjoy looks down at the
King, and in a "voice . . . imperial" bids him consider his ransom.
In reply, Henry admits that his army has been enfeebled by sickness,
but declares that the English advance will continue "Though
France herself and such another neighbor/Stood in our way." He
tosses Montjoy a purse of money for his "labor," then orders his
army to encamp beyond the river and be prepared to continue the
march next day. The scene concludes with a beautiful Turner-like
view of the English army marching wearily into the dusk alongside
the Picardy river.

For a few seconds the screen is in darkness as the Chorus
(voice-over) begins his solioquy: "Now entertain conjecture of a
time. . . ." Gradually, there is a fade-in to a long shot of the French
and English camps at night. Then, as the Chorus speech continues,
the camera tracks in to the French camp. The speech ends, a fanfare sounds, and the view dissolves to a close-up of the Constable's
star-adorned armor bedecking the inside of the French Dukes' tent.
The short scene that follows is a study in moods and tensions before
the battle. A pan shot reveals the Dukes seated impatiently but also
pensively at a dining table, awaiting the dawn of day. By contrast,
the Dauphin wanders excitedly around the tent, ludicrously eulogiz-
ing his horse and making boastful comments about the prisoners he
expects to capture. A sharp exchange between the blunt, realist
Constable and the fanciful, braggart Dauphin exposes their strained
relationship, and when the Prince withdraws to put on his armor,
the Constable amuses the other Dukes with cynical remarks about
the Dauphin's "valor." The emptiness of all the idle boasting and
cynicism is exposed by the sudden appearance of a messenger who
reveals that while they have been talking, the Lord Grandpré has,
most courageously, crept out into darkness and measured the distance to the English camp. As the scene concludes, the Dukes come
out of their tent, gaze at the lights of the English camp, and discuss
their shallow, misguided opinions of Henry and his countrymen.

Now follows a slow pan-shot across what is to be the battlefield:
from the French tents, past a distant view of Agincourt castle, over
to the English campfires. We hear the voice-over words of the

Chorus describing the "poor condemnèd English/ Like sacrifices, by their watchful fires." As the speech proceeds, the camera tracks in to the English camp from a high angle. When the Chorus starts to speak of the king, there is a sudden shift to a subjective viewpoint—it is Henry's as he moves about his camp. His shadow falls across an English soldier who is warming himself at a campfire. Through Henry's eyes we wander among the shadows of the English tents. And in the night scenes that follow, much of the shooting is from Henry's viewpoint; repeatedly it is his voice that we hear off-camera. The contrast here with the more objective presentation of the French camp is, of course, deliberate. The subjective shots increasingly emphasize Henry's intimacy with his men, his personal involvement with their fates, his identification with them: the English camp, seen through his eyes, is essentially part of him. Henry becomes, in effect, a new Chorus (replacing the original Chorus who will not be heard or seen again until the end of the picture), and the organizer and controller of most of what follows.

And now, as James Agee observes, Olivier's "adjustments and relationships of tone" make us subtly aware of the King's maturity and the rightness of his values. As an example, Agee refers to Henry's terse remarks on borrowing and returning Sir Thomas Erpingham's cloak: "the difference in tone between Olivier's almost schoolboyish "God-a-mercy" and his "Good old Knight," not long afterward, measures the King's growth in the time between with lovely strength, spaciousness, and cleanness . . . and psychologically or dramatically . . . it fully establishes the King's coming-of-age by raising honorable, brave, loyal, and dull old age (in Sir Thomas Erpingham) in the King's love and esteem to the level of any love he had ever felt for Falstaff."

In three successive scenes, the film discloses various attitudes to the king, the different states of mind of Henry's soldiers before the battle, and Henry's own doubts, fears and thoughts on conscience, responsibility and ceremony. Henry, temporarily incognito, first has an amusing encounter with Pistol. Next, he observes Fluellen ludicrously raising his voice at Gower in order to teach him the virtues of silence. Then he comes upon Williams, Court and Bates seated gloomily around a campfire, ruminating on the fate that awaits them on the morrow. This scene contains three of the film's finest vignette performances. Unforgettable is the pale, fearful, ingenuous face of the boy Court (Brian Nissen) as he utters his thoughts on the king's responsibility for those who die in his cause. Equally memorable is the contrast between the loyal, moderate, middle-aged Bates (Arthur Hambling) and the bitter, short-tempered young Williams (Jimmy Hanley) in their brief but pointed discussion with Henry. These characters, together with the others in the English camp, provide a representative sample of personalities—old and young, noble and humble, courageous, cynical and cowardly—and Henry's direct, personal involvements with all of them emphasize his popular, democratic qualities in sharp distinction to the aloofness of the aristocratic French.

Two moving soliloquies follow the campfire scene. Seated alongside the sleeping form of Court, Henry (his voice heard from off camera) delivers his speech on ceremony as the camera slowly tracks back to reveal the dawn rising on the day of reckoning. The morning light haloes Henry's face until it appears like an ivory mask peering out of a dark shroud. Moments later, outside a tent where a service is being conducted, Henry kneels and prays for the "God of battles" to "steel" his soldiers' hearts. These are the only occasions when he reveals any inner fears and doubts; they serve not to indicate hidden weaknesses but to show his lack of arrogance, his faith in God, his strength of character and selfless dedication to the Crown and his countrymen.

3. *Into Battle*

Now follows what is perhaps the most glorious display of pageantry ever to grace a motion picture screen. The darkness of the English camp fades into the brilliant blue of a tent flap adorned with the fleur-de-lys. This is swept aside to show the French Dukes, standing on a hilltop and being armed for the impending battle. Their spirit of jubilation is expressed in Bourbon's words: "The sun doth gild our armor!" Squires, servants, and lackeys swarm around them, offering their assistance. Then a page, bowing profusely, conducts them one by one past flowing banners and resplendent tents to their horses. It is like the preparations for a colorful tournament rather than the grim prelude to a battle. The scene dissolves to a close-up of the Cross of St. George, followed by the sight of a group of disconsolate English nobles standing armed and ready for Henry's command. In a mood of helplessness, the Earl of Westmoreland (Gerald Case) wishes that the meager English forces could be augmented with "But one ten thousand of those men in England/ That do not work today." In reply comes the voice of Henry off camera: "What's he that wishes so?" Henry, half-armored and leading his horse, strides into view. Rejecting Westmoreland's wish, he promptly counters such voices of despair with the rousing St. Crispin's Day speech. His words strike fire into the hearts of his men. As he speaks, soldiers of every rank crowd in upon him, eagerly, admiringly: their hearty cheers demonstrating that Henry and his army have become one—a band of brothers. In the forefront of his audience we observe the now enthusiastic Westmoreland, the dignified, loyal old Sir Thomas Erpingham, and the stalwart figures of Macmorris and Fluellen— all ready and willing to die, if necessary, for their beloved king. As in previous long speeches, the camera pulls away from Henry as his speech reaches its climax. But this time, as Henry mounts a cart to deliver his peroration, we see him in long shot at eye level —not diminished by a high angle shot as at Harfleur. Similarly, when, shortly afterwards, Henry receives Montjoy for the second time, the herald dismounts and Henry confronts him eye-to-eye and not from an inferior position.

A brief montage follows the Crispin's Day speech. Henry vaults blithely onto his horse. We see the English yeomen knocking rough-hewn sharpened stakes into the ground. Henry is being helped into his chainmail. The Dauphin is lowered onto his horse by a crane. A line of French drummers beats a tattoo. The French Dukes, in armor and on horseback, are joyfully downing goblets of wine. Meanwhile, arrows are being distributed to the English bowmen and other English soldiers are shown making their pointed stakes even sharper. Montjoy gallops up to Henry and offers him his second and last opportunity to surrender, a chance that Henry rejects in a proud and angry speech. The battle ensues.

Visually, the charge of the French cavalry is a climax built out of the alternation of a gathering momentum (the movement of the

French knights) with a tensed immobility (Henry's upraised sword, the line of English archers waiting with flexed longbows). This is the most exciting example in Western cinema of the application of the montage techniques first employed by Eisenstein in the Odessa Steps sequence of *The Battleship Potemkin*—the juxtaposing of powerful oppositions of lines, planes, angles, movement and stasis, order and chaos. The confrontation of a massive, ostentatious and unrestrained display of power by a small but disciplined and determined force symbolizes not only the film's contrast of French and English character but also the Nazi war machine stopped in its tracks by the dauntless few in that tight little island across the Channel. Hubert Clifford has described how the "momentum of the charge was enhanced by the cunningly mixed sound-track. A long cross-fade brought the music to the foreground, interchanging in prominence with the harness and armour-clanking sound effects as the charge gathered its impetus. The director very wisely suppressed the effects and allowed the music its full head as the climax approached." A succession of unforgettable images flashes across the screen:

(LS) The vast French army.

(LS) The handful of English troops.

(MS) French drummers beating a tattoo.

(LS) French crossbowmen marching up to their battle lines.

(CS) French banners being lowered.

(MS) Marshy water reflecting the French cavalry; horses' hoofs splashing through the mire. Dissolve to

(LS) Line of French cavalry in slow trot—the Constable in full armor visible in the foreground.

(MS) Line of English archers drawing and raising their bows.

(MCS) Henry on horseback—sword upraised like a conductor's baton.

(LS) Line of French cavalry quickening speed; their slow trot becomes an easy gallop then builds to a full charge.

(MS) English longbowmen taking aim.

(MS) (Low angle) Henry, glancing quickly from side to side, his sword held in readiness for signalling to his archers.

(LS) View of the charging French cavalry—seen through the lines of pointed stakes in the foreground of the picture.

(MS) English archers with drawn longbows.

(MS) Henry's sword slashing down.

(MCS) English archers firing their arrows.

(MLS) English archers firing their arrows.

(LS) View through the lines of pointed stakes as the deadly cloud of English arrows whizzes through the air and falls on the French cavalry. The charge is broken and confusion reigns among the French knights.

None of the later battle scenes is as impressive as this charge, and several are stylistically and tonally inconsistent with it. Thus a number of high angle shots following the charge show a curiously orderly mêlée that looks more like medieval paintings of a battle than the actual aftermath of the dynamic English counter-attack. A later scene, showing English soldiers dropping out of trees onto an unsuspecting band of French knights, seems a lark more appropriate to Errol Flynn and his merry men in *The Adventures of Robin Hood* (1938) than the kind of eyeball-to-eyeball strategies favored by Henry. As a panorama of chivalrous action, the battle is beautiful and bloodless; the only glimpse of blood in the entire sequence is that on the corpse of the English camp-boy slaughtered by the unchivalrous French who had fled from the battlefield.

Henry's triumph over the Constable in single combat confirms both the victory of the English and Henry's personal mastery of the situation. Now Montjoy, "his eyes . . . humbler than they us'd to be," solicits "charitable license" from Henry. On this, his third and last visit to Henry, he kneels at the King's feet; it is Henry's turn to look down upon the emissary of his defeated foes.

The beauty of the battle scenes carries over into the aftermath: in shots (more than a little reminiscent of the after-battle scenes in

Eisenstein's *Alexander Nevsky*) which show a riderless horse galloping over the deserted battlefield, and Henry's victorious troops winding in formal procession into Agincourt castle.

4. *After Agincourt*

There is a dissolve from a shot of the castle in the fall (St. Crispin's Day occurs on October 25) to the same view amid the snows of winter. The camera takes us into Agincourt village where Gower, Fluellen and Pistol reappear in a set that is an exact reproduction of the February illustration ("Village sous la neige") in *Les Très Riches Heures*. This is the film's best comedic episode, and its ironic reflection on the earlier single-combat scene is subtly pointed by Pistol's wearing of the Constable's breastplate while he is being humiliated by Fluellen.

A transition to the last big sequence of the film-within-a-play is made through a shot of the exterior of the French palace in springtime. This dissolves into an interior view of the palace—another formal composition showing a choir in the balcony, and below, in the audience chamber, the Duke of Burgundy (Valentine Dyall), his back to the window, flanked on one side by the English nobles (now dressed in their finery) and on the other by King Charles and his courtiers. Delivering Burgundy's great speech with grace and a tenderness that is underscored by Walton's lovely background music, Dyall turns and looks wistfully out across the countryside. The camera tracks out of the window and slowly pans through an uneven movement returning ultimately to an exterior view into the window—while Burgundy's words continue, a voice-over commentary on the landscape of France: "best garden of the world . . . corrupting in its own fertility." Here the visuals supply a superfluous and rather too picturesque objectification of Burgundy's images of neglect, ruin and devastation; they culminate ineffectively in a glimpse of two attractive children leaning over a fence—supposedly representing the savage state to which war reduces children.

This weak scene is followed by Henry's wooing of Katharine, an episode acted with consummate charm and skill. Olivier's performance as a lover promptly dispels any assumption that his range as an actor was limited to the grand style in which he had played the earlier scenes. His achievement here may be measured by his success in making the hitherto unfamiliar strategies of Henry the lover—his tour de force of false modesty and honeyed flattery—appear perfectly natural and appropriate to the warrior-king who was once the bosom companion of Falstaff.

The movements of Henry and Katharine in relation to the stylized setting effectively underscore the scene's dramatic developments. Thus, when Henry begins his wooing, the couple appear divided, in different panels—that is, an ornamental post stands between them. As Henry becomes more ardent, he moves into Katharine's panel. After Henry has offended Katharine by kissing her hand, the princess and Lady Alice retreat from him until they stand framed in separate windows; Henry joins them to stand in a third window so that the group forms an ornamental triptych rather than a natural arrangement. Then, Henry takes Katharine's hand, leads her away from the windows and panels that suggest their division and kisses her again, this time in the open set where nothing can separate them.

As Katharine and Henry are united, a joyous paean from the Chorus assists the surprise transition back to the Globe. Then—to the final and most glorious burst of Walton's music—the camera lifts us up, out of the playhouse to behold for the last time the spectacle of Elizabethan London, resplendent in the sunlight. A concluding long shot of the Tower affirms symbolically the permanence and strength of victorious England.

ADAPTED FROM SHAKESPEARE

Concerning the film's fidelity to its source, Olivier himself wrote "we made only a few minute alterations in the text and the cuts are even less than those invariably made in a stage production." (Program note, "The Filming of *Henry V*"). Many critics have echoed his words. Thus, Bosley Crowther, reviewing *Henry V* in *The New York Times* (June 18, 1946), stated "Olivier and his editor, Reginald Beck . . . have mounted the play with faithful service to the spirit and word." James Merton in *The Christian Science Monitor* (March 30, 1946) insisted that the film "follows the original text more closely than any of the many stage productions." While an anonymous reviewer in *Cue* magazine (June 15, 1946), maintained that "the film is faithful to Shakespeare's original in spirit and, almost invariably, in text." These admirable claims are, however, somewhat less than accurate. Examination of an uncut text of the play, the Pelican paperback edited by Alfred Harbage (to which all specific references to the play are made here), reveals that it contains some 3,199 lines. Collation of this text with the recently published film script of *Henry V* (see Bibliography) shows that Olivier retained only 1,505 lines of the original play. Speeches were abridged by cuts ranging from single words or phrases to many lines (e.g. "unwind your bloody flag" deleted at I.ii.101; all lines deleted at I.ii.106–121, 136–221). Whole scenes were virtually omitted (e.g., 177 out of 193 lines were excluded from II.ii; 107 out of 120 lines were removed from IV.viii).

The material removed falls into at least six categories: (1) background, including both antecedent action and foreshadowing of events that follow the action of the play; (2) much elaboration of idea, argument and detail; (3) all suggestions that England is endangered by internal conspiracy or that Scotland is a potential threat; (4) much material involving the comic characters; (5) passages and incidents revealing aspects of Henry's character unlikely to be attractive to modern audiences; (6) miscellaneous material involving the French, including lines that show the French nobles to be more spirited, worthy adversaries than the rather weak, brash figures they are made to appear in the film.

Excluded background material involves the detailing of earlier history (as at I.ii. 106–121) and the anticipation of the disasters of Henry VI's reign (Final Chorus 7–13). The exclusion of certain passages elaborating upon details or ideas is exemplified by the omission of I.ii.60–64, II.iv.16–22, and IV.viii.79–95. The removal of I.ii.136–221, II. Chor. 20–29 and most of II.ii.1–39, 48–187 excludes from the film all references to the problem of the Scots and the whole episode of the traitors (Cambridge, Scroop and Grey) and their condemnation. The abridgement of material relating to the comic characters results in the omission of much of Pistol's bombast in II.i, the cordial end to the quarrel of Nym and Pistol at II.i.101–112, the Boy's long speech on the characters of Bardolph, Pistol and Nym and his decision to leave them (III.ii.25–49), the cause of Pistol's quarrel with Fluellen and the latter's refusal to save Bardolph from hanging for the crime of stealing a pax (III.vi), and the scene of Pistol holding a French prisoner to ransom (IV.iv).

The deletions affecting Henry's character are extensive; they involve the omission of exaggerated claims about his perfection and prowess (I.i.30–31, 38–53; and Fluellen's comparison of Henry with Alexander the Great at IV.vii.20–48); Henry's tirade before the gates of Harfleur, threatening dire consequences to the besieged if they refuse to surrender the city (III.iii.3–43); Henry's bragging about English superiority to the French (III.vi.141–147) and his citing of the French as bad neighbors who teach the English what is needful (IV.i.3–12); his argument that war is *God's* vengeance and also an opportunity for the individual to prepare himself against damnation (IV.i.149–175); his exchange of gages with Michael Williams in the expectation of taking up their quarrel after the battle (IV.i.195–209); his listing of all that he has done to atone for his father's usurpation of the throne (IV.i.278–292); his order to execute all the French prisoners (IV.vii.55–60); his boasting to Fluellen about his Welsh birth (IV.vii.87–109); his passing of the gage to the unsuspecting Fluellen, and the end of the "prank" (IV.viii.1–67); his allusion to Kate, during the wooing scene, as a good "soldier-breeder" who will produce a boy "that shall go to Constantinople and take the Turk by the beard" (V.ii.197–204), and his discussion with Burgundy concerning Kate, virgins and the "virgin cities" of France.

Omitted passages concerning the French include King Charles's allusions to the ferocity of the English and the strength of Henry's army (II.iv.9–14, 48–50); the Dauphin's defiant reply to Henry's ambassador (II.iv.127–131); Orleans' objections to the Constable's ironic comments about the Dauphin's valor (III.vii. 105–120); the arrogant and disparaging comments of the Constable and Grandpré about the "poor and starved band" of English (IV.ii.15–32, 41–59); and Montjoy's request to book and bury the dead so that the "vulgar" do not "drench their peasant limbs/ In blood of princes. . . ." (IV.vii.69–78).

It must be emphasized that the omission of what amounts to 1,694 lines or some 50% of the original text is only one of several ways in which the text of the film script differs from the uncut text of the play. There is also considerable transposition of material (mainly affecting the Chorus speeches); there are some additions, amounting to at least sixteen lines; and there are minor substitutions of familiar, modern words for archaic, unfamiliar ones.

Olivier's changes affecting the Chorus may be summarized as follows:

> Prologue: loses lines 15–17, 24–25
> Act II Chorus is reduced to II Chorus 1–11 plus a conflation of part of II Chor. 31 and 39–40:
>> "Linger your patience on, for, if we may
>> We'll not offend one stomach with our play."
> Following II.i is provided a "new" Chorus speech consisting of II Chor. 31–32 and 34–42 (with brief omissions).
> Following II.ii is provided a "new" Chorus speech consisting of III Chor. 34–35.
> Following II.iii is provided a "new" Chorus speech consisting of III Chor. 1–5, 7–15, 17, 19–20, 22–24 and II Chor. 12–15.
> III Chorus is reduced to lines 25–27.
> Following III.ii.22 ("bate thy rage!") is provided a "new" Chorus speech consisting of III Chor. 32–34.
> Following III.vi is provided a "new" Chorus speech consisting of IV Chor. 1–14, 17–22 (". . . away").
> IV Chorus is reduced to 15–16, 23–34, 43–47.
> V Chorus is omitted.
> The Final Chorus is reduced to 1–6, 13–14.

Aside from changes affecting the Chorus, other transpositions include:

> I.ii.22 relocated to follow I.ii.23.
> II.i.34–35 ("O well-a-day . . . committed.") transposed to follow II.i.77.
> III.ii.109–110 transposed to follow III.ii.94.
> III.vi.66–68 (". . . such"), 76–77 (". . . of the camp . . . thought on.") transposed to follow V.i.12.
> IV.v.8–12 and 20–24 transposed to follow IV.vi.2.

In addition, certain lines have been reassigned to different characters, resulting in the omission of several minor characters and the creation of a new one (the Duke of Berri) who does not actually appear in Shakespeare's play. These changes are as follows:

> I.ii.100–105 ("Gracious lord . . . Prince.") Lines taken from Canterbury and given to Exeter.

I.ii.122–125 Taken from Exeter and given to Salisbury. The French Ambassador's lines are divided between Montjoy the Herald (who speaks I.ii.238–240) and the Duke of Berri (who speaks the remaining lines of the Ambassador.)

In II.iv. the Dukes of Britaine and Brabant are omitted.

In III.v. the Duke of Britaine is omitted but the Dukes of Bourbon and Orleans appear. Britaine's lines (III.v.10–14) are given to Bourbon. The Constable's lines (III.v.15–18) are given to Orleans. The Dauphin's lines (III.v.27–31) are given to Bourbon.

In III.vii. Bourbon replaces Lord Rambures. Rambures' lines are distributed among Orleans, the Dauphin and Bourbon. Williams' lines (IV.i.127–137) are given to the Boy (Court).

IV.ii. Bourbon replaces Rambures and Beaumont.

The most notable textual additions are (1) the death of Falstaff scene, consisting of thirteen lines inserted after II.ii, and (2) the last three lines uttered by Pistol as he bids farewell to Mistress Quickly (end of II.iii). The Falstaff episode consists of lines taken from the final scene of 2 *Henry IV;* while Pistol's farewell is an adaptation of words spoken by Tamburlaine in Marlowe's play, *Tamburlaine the Great,* Part I, act II, scene v.

Substitutions of modern words for archaic ones are few in number; a typical example is Olivier's replacement of *pop-gun* for *elder-gun* in Williams' line, "That's a perilous shot out of an elder gun" (IV.i. 186–187.)

The foregoing summary of differences between the film script and Shakespeare's play does not, of course, explain the reasons for them. And a study as brief as this cannot account for all the omissions, changes and adaptations. However, some generalizations can be made. Olivier evidently excluded some of the background material for several reasons: to simplify the story for audiences unfamiliar with English history and with the place of *Henry V* in Shakespeare's English history cycle; to focus on the glorious episode that is climaxed by the battle of Agincourt as a series of events that form a complete story, not a narrative that is part of a larger context; to remove Renaissance concepts of kingship, hierarchy and politics that are unlikely to be received with understanding or sympathy by modern "democratic" audiences; and to eliminate the potentially static (i.e. nonfilmic) quality inherent in the long speeches in which much background material occurs.

Much of the elaboration of idea, argument and detail was reduced in the interest of preparing a taut, concise, fluent script, avoiding lengthy visual concentration on any single character and allowing considerable freedom for camerawork and editing. And also implicit in the reduction of that kind of material is a concession to the difficulty audiences often meet in comprehending complex arguments and ideas expressed through film dialogue.

In his article, "Adapted from a Play by W. Shakespeare," (*Hollywood Quarterly* II, October 1946), James E. Phillips argues plausibly that the discussion of the problem of Scotland is excluded because of its unpalatable "totalitarian flavor" and because it embodies "an elaborate analysis of England's political structure and Henry's place in it . . . [which] means little to the citizens of [modern] democracies." It also seems to have been removed because it suggests a lack of unity against the common enemy. Olivier's *Henry V* was an expression of the solidarity of Britain in 1944: the nation in its finest hour had become a "band of brothers." Inclusion of the material relating to the problem of Scotland would have undermined this idea. Thus, the film deliberately ignores Scotland's existence—in the fifteenth century—as a separate kingdom and a potential military threat to the English. But it pointedly retains the scene of the four captains (III.ii.50–129) in which the Scotsman, Captain Jamy ("a marvelous falorous gentleman") appears as one of the symbols of the unity of the "four kingdoms" under the monarchy of Henry. Similarly, Henry's scene with the conspirators was probably eliminated not only because, as James Phillips maintains, it developed Elizabethan political ideas that are unfamiliar and even objectionable to modern audiences, but also because, in 1944, it could have been interpreted as an allusion to the existence of a well-organized fifth column.

Much of the comedic material appears to have been abridged to make the comedy more visual and less verbal. Pistol's bombast, some of which is difficult to comprehend without close acquaintance with the text, has been drastically cut, while Pistol himself is interpreted by Robert Newton as a character given to grandiose flourishes and grotesque grimaces and movements. The other comic characters are reduced virtually to slapstick figures which have obvious parallels in film comedy. This reduction is assisted by the elimination of most material exposing their more serious or unsavory aspects and fates. They are funny without being corrupting influences. There is no cancer, comedic or otherwise, in the England of Olivier's Henry, and to make sure that we are aware of it, Olivier shows Falstaff, the high-priest of comedy and corruption, on his deathbed, being rejected by the king. The first comic scene (II.i.) is retained largely because it provides a comic parallel to the scene before Agincourt in which Henry quarrels with Michael Williams. Significantly, Olivier cuts the cordial end to the quarrel of Pistol and Nym, leaving their differences unresolved just as the quarrel of Henry and Williams is left unsettled in the film. Throughout both play and film, Pistol functions as a kind of comic alter ego of Henry. The other comic characters, functionally less important than Pistol, are not seen after III.i. But Pistol reappears as a coward whose harmless braggadocio is displayed first in contrast with Henry's magnificent charge into the breach before Harfleur, then before Agincourt in a brief but ludicrous encounter with "Harry le Roy," and finally in the treatment he receives at the hand of Fluellen. Olivier deleted Henry's ferocious threat of pillage, rape and murder (III.iii) but retained Pistol as the sole English coward and looter. English audiences were thus invited to laugh at his cowardice while seeing themselves flatteringly mirrored in the characters of the "happy few" who fought at Agincourt.

The most consequential changes are, of course, those affecting the main character. As James Phillips points out, Henry has been modernized so that he appeals to "audiences apathetic about kingship but particularly susceptible to the heroic glamor that surrounds a brilliant and successful military leader." This modernization involves a transformation of Henry from an ideal Renaissance monarch into a dynamic personality who "possesses, above all things, leadership in the modern, military sense of the term. He demonstrates in practically all respects the qualities attributed to the ideal officer by current Service journals." He also apotheosizes most of the public school virtues that were supposed to have built the British Empire. "He has assurance, poise, and self-confidence in every situation, whether it be attack or retreat in war or in love." A no-nonsense professional, he "carries himself with authority and dresses impressively. . . . He instills an enthusiasm and inspires a courage like his own in those about him. . . . Without sacrificing dignity or authority, he maintains the proper comradely relationship with subordinates and inferiors. In a word, he is a figure completely recognizable and completely understandable today."

Many of Henry's qualities remind us of the now almost mythical R.A.F. heroes of the Battle of Britain (typified by the late Richard Hillary), or, perhaps more appropriate to Olivier himself, of valiant officers in the Fleet Air Arm. Henry's back-to-the-wall defiance, his courage and tenacity are accompanied by likeable displays of casualness and sportsmanship that are seldom evident in Shakespeare's king. Thus, early in the film we see Henry toss aside his crown (as if throwing his hat onto a hatrack) as he announces preparations for war; and in a later scene, by contrast to the French knights who, rather helplessly, have to be hoisted onto their mounts, Henry leaps nimbly onto his charger. Olivier's drastic cutting of II.ii leaves little more to that scene than the episode in which Henry shows his sporting magnanimity towards the drunkard who railed against him. Passages indicating Henry's ruthlessness have been omitted, but Olivier retains the scene in which the king discovers the murder of the camp boys ("I was not angry since I came to France/ Until this instant"): in 1944 it had pointed relevance to Nazi atrocities. He follows this with an entirely new scene in which Henry, infuriated with what he has witnessed, rides into battle and takes on the Constable of France in single combat.

Exaggerated claims about Henry's character and abilities, such as those made by the prelates in I.i, have been excluded from the film. True, Olivier's Henry is an idealized figure, but the ideal qualities he possesses are made credible to modern audiences because they are fully manifest in his actions, not simply attributed to him by others. This Henry constantly demonstrates the kind of man he is. And to a considerable extent he is a showman, an organizer, a public man. Again and again we see him addressing audiences within the film—speaking to them from his throne, or astride his horse, or from a wagon that he uses as a platform; we see him controlling the embarkation from Southampton, directing the battle of Agincourt like the conductor of an orchestra, and putting on a well-prepared solo performance for Kate to whom he makes love in public. Except in his brief soliloquies before Agincourt, Olivier's

Henry shows himself to be a thorough-going extrovert, an almost entirely externalized image of a hero. Gone is Shakespeare's more complex portrait of an autocratic monarch who, after being eulogized for his wisdom, justice and chivalry, threatens the besieged citizens of Harfleur with murder, rape and pillage and orders the execution of French prisoners-of-war and who, at other times, broods, conscience-stricken over his father's usurpation of the throne. Olivier's Henry reveals no difficult contradictions of character or reputation, and his dynamism and charm almost compel us to forget that he is really too good to be true. Moreover, as Phillips also notices, enhancing Henry's irresistibly attractive qualities is the fact that—unlike so many modern leaders—he is "inevitably successful. In truth, no really serious obstacles are ever put in his way, so that in the film, even more than in the play, his French expedition becomes a patriotic lark for the delight and wonder of all." Phillips sums up his character as one who "excites admiration without demanding reference to the nation which he heads, the institution [i.e. the monarchy] which he represents, or the cause which he champions." He is, in short, a charming and plausibly dynamic individualist, somewhat reminiscent at times of the daredevil young Winston Churchill as he emerges from the pages of *My Early Life,* and also, at times, recalling traditional heroes of Westerns whose rugged individualism and inevitable triumph over their adversaries have become clichés in countless movies from Bronco Billy to John Wayne.

Where Henry's character has been simplified in order to emphasize his positive, heroic and virtuous qualities, Olivier's simplification of the French has the opposite purpose and effect. Notwithstanding the French show of power and the apparent military weakness of the English, we are never left in doubt as to the outcome of the conflict. The French nobles are, clearly, not the kind of men who win battles. In the film (if not in the play) Henry never boasts. He does, indeed, "speak proudly" on many occasions, but his deeds always fulfill his words. By contrast, Olivier shows the French nobles to be drinkers and boasters, not men of action. They sit at table discussing the character of the English while Henry continues his advance into France. They gamble before the battle for prisoners they have not yet taken. Their king, unlike Shakespeare's

King Charles, is portrayed as a nervous and spiritless dotard who wilts and faints upon hearing the threats uttered by Henry's ambassador. Charles's son, the Dauphin, treated by the king as if he were a petulant child, shows excessive vanity and presumption before Agincourt and cowardice during the actual battle. Of the French nobles who are characterized, only the Constable of France is shown to be a realist and a man of spirit. It is the Constable who warns the Dauphin not to underestimate Henry (II.iv.29–33), who cynically mocks the Dauphin's vanity on the night before Agincourt, and who seeks out and engages Henry in single combat during the battle. He is, like Pistol, a figure of contrast. Where Pistol is shown to be virtually the only coward in an army of English heroes, the Constable appears as the only French noble who has courage and lacks arrogance.

The transpositions and deletions affecting the Chorus primarily concern not character but the gradual movement from the theatrical (Globe Theatre setting) to the cinematic, and the need for effective filmic transitions between certain scenes. In the Prologue the Chorus asks dubiously:

> Can this cockpit hold
> The vasty fields of France? Or may we cram
> Within this wooden O the very casques
> That did affright the air at Agincourt?

The answer, of course, is: Not in Shakespeare's theatre. But Olivier's *Henry V* is a film and film techniques obviate the need for a Chorus to indicate transitions in time and space or to describe what cannot be shown within the limitations of a theatre. Appropriately, in the Globe setting the Chorus speeches function exactly as they do in Shakespeare's play. But their distribution and substance change along with their functions as the story moves out of the confines of the Globe Theatre. Following II.i, a "new" Chorus speech is used to effect the transition from the stylized theatrical scene (the Globe curtain to which the Chorus directs our attention) to the more naturalistic, more filmic scene (Henry at Southampton) —after which transition the Chorus for the first time becomes a disembodied voice. Olivier then begins using the Chorus filmically rather than theatrically. That is, gradually, the Chorus is turned into something like a documentary film commentator. His speeches are cut and transposed until what remains is not verbal description so much as purely atmospheric language, or a means of effecting smooth transitions between scenes that contrast sharply in style or mood, or commentary that reinforces and enlarges the visuals or stands in ironic relationship to them.

A brief example of the filmic use of the Chorus is Olivier's treatment of the following passage from III Chor. 32–33:

> . . . and the nimble gunner
> With linstock now the devilish cannon touches,
> And down goes all before them.

In the play these lines are delivered by the Chorus immediately before Henry's great speech at Harfleur (III.i). Olivier has shifted them so that they follow the scene in which Fluellen drives Pistol and his comrades into the breach (III.ii) and precede the scene of the four captains. In their original context the lines are part of a longer passage in which the Chorus invites the audience to work their thoughts and "therein see a siege. . . ." But Olivier has removed them for use as off-camera commentary in conjunction with two shots: (1) a close-up of a flaming linstock touching the gunpowder box of a cannon which then fires, (2) a medium shot of a wall being blown down. The words and pictures do not merely repeat each other. The pictures show specifically what is generalized in the words; they endow them with more realism than they would normally possess. On the other hand, the words give wider significance to what is shown on the screen. We are not simply observing one cannon shooting down a wall. We understand that what we are witnessing is the skill of the English gunners and the power of their weapons—so that when (in III.iii) the Governor of Harfleur refers to "so great a siege," he does not seem to be exaggerating. Taken together the pictures and the speech that accompanies them are a concise and economic way of providing atmosphere. All the violence of the siege is expressed simply in Henry's "Once more unto the breach. . . ." and the little scene of the "devilish cannon" demolishing a wall. Dramatically, the scene serves as a substitute for a deleted speech (the Boy's soliloquy denouncing the corruption of Nym, Pistol and Bardolph) and like that speech it bridges two different scenes involving Fluellen, scenes that would contrast awkwardly if juxtaposed. In other words, the burst of cannon fire and the verbal imagery that accompanies it ease the film's sudden shift from the violent slapstick of Fluellen's assault on Pistol to the milder humor of the captains' scene.

The Chorus is, of course, used for more important transitions. Some of them are purely atmospheric, as in the use of IV Chor. 1–14 ("Now entertain conjecture of a time . . .") to shift the scene from the English army marching wearily along the Picardy river to a view of the French and English camps at night. Other choric passages are used to make ironic commentaries (not always inherent in their original contexts) upon the scenes they introduce, as in the use of II Chor. 12–15 ("The French . . . Shake in their fear . . .") as the camera discloses a group of lethargic, indifferent French nobles. Yet other passages are so placed as to shape attitudes to specific characters, as in the transposition of IV Chor. 17–22 (". . . The confident and over-lusty French . . .") so that it immediately precedes the scene in the Duke of Orleans' tent (III.vii). In general, the choric material has been woven anew into the fabric of the screenplay.

STYLES IN CONFLICT?

Much controversy has centered on the visual styles of *Henry V*. There is no critical agreement as to what the various styles are, whether they are integrated, or whether they are relevant to an adaptation of Shakespeare. Thus, James Agee comments: "The Battle of Agincourt is not realistic. Olivier took great care not to make it so." (*Time*, April 8, 1946). And Siegfried Kracauer states: "The battle in *Henry V* . . . is just a decorative pageant." (*Theory of Film*, 1971 ed., p. 227). By contrast, George W. Linden observes: "The actual battle scenes, with the crosscutting from the French noblemen to the ungentlemanly English longbowmen and their rain of arrows, are highly 'realistic' and exciting." (*Reflections on the Screen*, 1970, p. 22). Kracauer implies that the styles are both integrated and relevant: ". . . the opening scenes of Olivier's *Henry V* . . . [do] credit to Olivier's film sense. . . . [They are] an attempt to put the theatrical spectacle in brackets and offset the effect of its stylizations by a touch of camera reality." (*Theory of*

Film, p. 260.) Richard Griffith is even more explicit in insisting that the styles are unified and justified: *"Henry V* . . . was probably the first instance of a legitimately photographed play, inasmuch as its structure was designed constantly to remind the spectator of the fact that it was a play and not a film. When the action moved out of the Globe Theatre it moved into fairyland, not actuality, and thus avoided that conflict between poetic speech and three-dimensional reality that has set previous versions of Shakespeare at nought." ("The Film Since Then," in Paul Rotha's *The Film Till Now,* 1967 ed., p. 560.) Linden's reactions contradict both Kracauer and Griffith. After arguing that the battle is "realistic"—although "it presents . . . a panorama of action . . . with a unity and coherence that no one involved in the actual battle could hope to match"—he continues: "This is followed by a shock. Henry goes to woo the fair Katharine. Their courting scene is magnificent, but he woos in a phony castle. The plains, the flying banners, the rain of arrows, the falling warriors have all given us a strong illusion of reality and three dimensions; suddenly we are confronted by cardboard castles and the screen image falls flat. Olivier has mistakenly mixed theatrical props with film reality and they don't fit." (*Reflections on the Screen,* p. 22.) More bluntly than Linden, an anonymous reviewer for *P.M. New York* (January 16, 1946) remarks that "The words . . . are Shakespeare's, but the costumes and settings [are] . . . 'early Cecil B. De Mille'" while James Agate in the London *Times* (December 3, 1944) dismisses most of the film as stylistically irrelevant to the play: "All the early part struck me as enchanting. But when the film flew, so to speak, out of the window, Shakespeare, as far as I am concerned, walked out of the door."

These disagreements are partly the result of a failure to sort out which styles are discernible and how they relate to the dramatic material, and partly to a failure to cope with the apparent incongruity of the same actors reappearing in different stylistic settings. Most commentators assume that there are only two styles in the film. But in fact at least three can be distinguished: (1) the anti-illusionistic theatrical, (2) the quasi-naturalistic, and (3) the illusionistic-stylized.

1. Anti-illusionistic theatrical. This style is evident in the framing scenes in the Globe Theatre. Olivier not only presents a some-

what flamboyant performance, he also destroys its theatrical illusion for the *movie* audience by displaying the "artificialities" of the show (costumes, make-up, etc.) in relation to the "real" (theatre) audience, and by disclosing how everything "works"—taking us behind the stage into the greenroom, showing us boys dressed as women, Henry clearing his throat before making his entrance, the sound effects man almost missing a cue from the Archbishop. Curiously, although what we are watching is a theatrical performance, the total effect is that of a process documentary film. It is not surprising to hear that these scenes have been excerpted and shown to schoolchildren as a film on "How plays were staged in Shakespeare's time." James Agee's objection to the "subtly patronizing way in which a good deal" of the opening sequence was done shows, aside from its irrelevant criticism, an awareness of stylistic differences between this part of the film and the scenes that follow it. In general, the opening and closing scenes of *Henry V* lack stylization and are closer to the naturalistic than the remainder of the film.

2. Quasi-naturalistic. Following the opening sequence, this is the style of most of the film apart from the scenes in the French palace and the final return to the theatre setting. Here the style that predominates is apparently naturalistic, but it is actually something more than that: a kind of tidied-up or "prettified" naturalism. Thus we see what appears to be a real ship at a real quayside in Southampton, or Henry confronting Montjoy in a real landscape. But such scenes are improved in a variety of ways through the photographer's art—by careful composition, by choice of angle, soft focus, lighting, etc., that enhances the natural appearance of what is being shown. Again and again Olivier and his cameraman (Robert Krasker) seem to be creating the effect of beautiful paintings out of the natural scene, as in the Turner-like landscape through which the weary English army marches into the dusk, or the almost Pre-Raphaelite scene revealing Henry's cloaked form, beside the campfire, delivering his soliloquy on Ceremony as the dawn breaks slowly in the background. Linden has come close to indicating the stylistic nature of such quasi-naturalistic scenes in describing the Agincourt battle as "a panorama of action . . . with a unity and coherence that no one involved in the actual battle could hope to match, let alone actors on a stage."

3. Illusionistic-stylized. Most of the controversy has been aroused by those scenes which look like pre-Renaissance paintings. Linden, as we have seen, dismisses such scenes as "phony . . . cardboard castles . . . theatrical props," while Agee refers to the "French court, in fragility and elegance, spaciousness and color . . . [as] probably the most enchanting single set ever to appear on the screen." These settings look artificial, and are, of course, intended to look that way. Their stylization reproduces the stylization of the medieval illustrations on which they are based. The usual objections to them are that they seem out of place in relation to real actors and that they jar with the other visual styles in the same film. Both objections are based on a lack of understanding, which, curiously, does not usually extend to Hollywood musicals where singers and dancers are frequently shown in highly unrealistic or stylized settings and which often contain extreme contrasts of visual style—especially when the musical sequences are embedded in a narrative. It is generally realized that in musicals settings can relate to moods expressed by the music. They can do more than that. Such films as Fellini's *Juliet of the Spirits* (1965) strikingly demonstrate how settings and costumes can be used as projections of the mental states of characters in the story. And those settings in *Henry V* that Linden dismisses as "phony" are in fact used by Olivier to express or shape attitudes to character and situation.

The scenery against which King Charles and his courtiers move helps to reinforce the impression that the French are essentially out of touch with reality. The settings have a fairy-tale-like quality and a frail elegance that is sharply contrasted with the more naturalistic scenery and real landscapes in which Henry and his army appear. Appropriately, the unreal French court is first shown to us as a complement to these words of the Chorus:

> The French, advis'd by good intelligence
> Of this most dreadful preparation [of Henry's army]
> Shake in their fear, and with pale policy,
> Seek to divert the English purposes.

In a later scene, Henry at the head of his army addresses the Governor of Harfleur who has appeared on the city wall. Here the weakness of the French is emphasized in the contrast between the full-size naturalistic English army and the out-of-proportion-and-perspective medieval style wall from which the Governor surrenders his city. Linden has specifically objected to an even later contrast between what he calls the "realistic" battle scenes and Henry's wooing of Katharine in a "phony castle." But this contrast is perfectly appropriate. The realistic battlefield is *Henry's* world where he confronts the French with their hour of truth; the unreal palace is *Katharine's* world, and to woo and win her on her own ground Henry attempts what is unreal to him: the gallantries and flatteries of the courtly lover.

Even in the quasi-naturalistic scenes, Olivier has a tendency to develop almost formal pictorial arrangements, but characters appearing in such scenes are never reduced to mere elements within a picture. Thus, when Henry rides out to engage the Constable in single combat, we see, to the right of the screen, a close-up of a sword with its blade stuck in the soil of the battlefield, while to the left, at long-shot distance, Henry is galloping furiously into the fray. Momentarily, Henry seems merely part of the pictorial design of the shot, but he swiftly moves out of the ornamental arrangement which can then be seen to have had a symbolic rather than a purely pictorial function. By contrast, the scenes in the French court show a reductive tendency in the treatment of character in relation to pictorial design. Characters in those scenes are usually disclosed in formal poses or moving into formal arrangements in relation to the stylized scenery until they appear like illustrations within panels formed by the scenic structures. Again and again, windows, or struts and poles that form part of the scenery become the frames or outlines of pictures that contain separate characters. Thus we see the Dauphin and the English ambassador placed in separate panels by their movement into a position on either side of a scenery brace. Burgundy delivers his great speech situated between the English and the French courtiers, a formal grouping of the actors that reduces them to extensions of the stylized scenery.

At Agincourt, where the setting is generally a quasi-naturalistic one for both sides, the pageantry of the French contrasts with the English army's honest-to-God lack of ostentation. While Henry is the only showman among the English, the entire French army seems, unrealistically, to be more involved in putting on a gigantic entertainment, a super-tournament, than in fighting a battle. The tents of the French nobles are fantastically decorated with ornamental gables and other ostentatious displays. There is an impressive parade of drummers, a ceremonious procedure in which pages conduct knights to their horses, an elaborate demonstration of hoisting a heavily-armored noble into his beautifully caparisoned saddle (cross-cut with a shot of Henry being helped into a simple chain-mail coat), and, of course, a magnificently decorative charge preceded by a colorful display of banners. In the English camp, on the other hand, the emphasis is on down-to-earth practical preparations. No parades, no shows, but a line of archers sharpening stakes and receiving supplies of arrows. Significantly, Olivier focuses exclusively on the nobles when he concentrates on the French; when he shifts our attention to the English camp we see soldiers of all ranks and memorable scenes in which Henry, his nobles and yeoman-subjects mingle in a free, casual and comradely manner. Patently, the French are depicted as vainglorious, impractical and aristocratic, while the English are shown to be sober, realistic, practical and democratic.

MUSIC

The film contains a variety of musical styles in addition to its range of visual styles. In an analysis of Walton's score for *Henry V*, Hubert Clifford comments: "The form of the film posed an awkward problem for the composer—the conflict between three periods. With the resources of 1944 (for the ears of 1944), the composer had to encompass a musical atmosphere of the days of Queen Elizabeth [I] and those of Henry V. Walton's solution of the problem was as satisfactory as any stylistic compromise of this kind could be. Apart from the use in certain sequences of plainsong and organum and of the Agincourt Song, Walton's method was to divide the dramatic atmosphere and express it in terms of his own musical mind. The result was a happy absence of the ersatz . . . [In] *Henry V* there was an authentic English musical voice. . . ." (From an article quoted in John Huntley, *British Film Music,* n.d., pp. 74–75.)

In the introductory playhouse scenes Walton conveys the idiom of Elizabethan theatre music by imitating its style and instrumentation. What Dr. Clifford refers to as a division of dramatic atmosphere is discernible in the changes of musical style following the opening scenes. The changes relate to a variety of musical functions in addition to or aside from the limited one of "period reproduction." There is, first of all, music used simply to suggest or create moods, as for example, the two lovely melodic passages scored exclusively for strings: "Passacaglia—The Death of Falstaff" and "Touch her soft lips and part" (Pistol's farewell to the Hostess). Neither of these pieces has any stylistic or idiomatic identity with the period music of the playhouse. Walton also uses nonperiod music to convey a sense of locale, for example, in his poignant adaptation of the Auvergne folk song "Baleiro" as an accompaniment to the Duke of Burgundy's speech, during which the camera wanders over the devastated French countryside. Then there are the numerous fanfares used to herald the start of a new scene or the arrival of an important personage, as in the Duke of Exeter's appearance at the court of King Charles before the Harfleur scenes. Walton's choral and orchestral version of the traditional "Agincourt Song" with its words by sixteenth century English poet Michael Drayton, recasts the simple, original tune into an almost timeless paean—a song of thanksgiving and triumph that is meant to belong to 1945 as much as to 1415, and which is comparable functionally and stylistically with the joyful "Hallelujah" that concludes Walton's oratorio, *Belshazzar's Feast* (1931).

It is, of course, Walton's music for the battle of Agincourt that departs most radically from the musical style of the playhouse scenes. What we hear in that sequence is not period reproduction, simple mood music, the adaptation of traditional or folk melodies or, mercifully, anything resembling the kind of battle music that is typical of Hollywood epics, but instead a musical language that is new to cinema: the symphonic voice of William Walton himself. It is the language that can be heard in his first symphony (1935) as well as in passages of such orchestral overtures as *Crown Imperial* (1937) and *Orb and Sceptre* (1953). In these nonfilmic compositions the music is nonprogrammatic but nevertheless suggests qualities one associates with the word *chivalry* and also with Elgar's favorite term, *nobilemente*. In particular, the opening movement of Walton's first symphony, which, as James Lyons says, has a "neoclassic" utterance that is "uncompromisingly modern in its syntax," anticipates the sounds and rhythms of the Agincourt music and deserves close comparison with it. Such a task is, however, beyond the scope of this short study.

Muir Mathieson has noticed how in the Agincourt sequence "it was left to the music to build up the tension," [Note to phonograph recording, Sir William Walton, *Music from Shakespearean Films,* Angel record 36198] while Dr. Clifford has pointed out that "The director very wisely suppressed the [sound] effects and allowed the music its full head as the climax was approached." Under the direction of Henry's sword-baton, the sound effects return with the flight of arrows that actually provides the climax to the music. This montage of visuals, music and sound effects achieves the audiovisual synthesis that Eisenstein and Prokofiev had attempted less successfully in the battle on the ice sequence in *Alexander Nevsky* (1938). Eisenstein was unwilling to let us forget for one moment that we are watching a conflict between ruthless Teutonic knights and valiant Russians. His fusion of music, sound effects and visuals tend to express mood and to shape attitudes rather than to create a total dramatic effect. Thus he breaks the tension and disrupts the coherence of the sequence to show us one of his Russian superheroes polishing off the Teutons as easily as if he were felling a tree. And Prokofiev accompanies this sudden shift to the ludicrous-comedic by passages of jaunty dance-like music that sound out of place in the midst of a battle. By contrast, Olivier and Walton subordinate each separate element—music, visuals, sound effects—to the development of a single, dominant effect which is not interrupted until it has reached its climax. The splendor and rhythm of the charge becomes more important than the significance of the conflict or any attitude towards the French. Apropos of this, Dr. Clifford recalls that when the film was first shown, the Agincourt sequence "provoked the sophisticated press-showing audience to an ovation." He adds: "I suspect the audience did not realise that they were applauding 't'other side' but no matter. . . . The result was a tour-de-force."

THE DIRECTOR'S VOICE

Whether or not the propagandist elements of *Henry V* conflict with its aesthetic qualities now seems an academic question; it has always troubled the public less than the critics. Audiences have, time and again, enjoyed the film without being aware of its partially propagandist purpose. And probably many of the critics who objected would have been unaware of it also if the film had been made at any other time. However, as the events of the Second World War recede from us, the picture has come to seem less overtly chauvinistic than, say, *Alexander Nevsky,* less propagandist than *The Birth of a Nation, The Battleship Potemkin, Triumph of the Will,* and *The Great Dictator*—all of which have won frequent critical acclaim as examples of motion picture art.

A more significant question is whether *Henry V* is merely an adaptation or whether it embodies a personal statement by its director. Certainly Shakespeare purists could marshal convincing evidence that the picture is sometimes but not always Shakespeare. The language, themes, plot, and to some extent the characterizations are Shakespeare's, but the message of the film, at least in part, is Olivier's. *Henry V* is, ultimately, a movie about the strengths of discipline, determination, leadership and union in a common cause, and the hollowness of arrogance, ostentation and indecision. Where Shakespeare, in the words of James E. Phillips, "sets up the framework for his portrait of Henry as an ideal ruler according to Renaissance standards," Olivier's emphases and omissions give *Henry V* a significance that transcends its original national or patriotic considerations. It is no coincidence that Olivier described *Hamlet,* his next picture, as the tragedy of "a man who could not make up his own mind." By contrast, Olivier used the chronicle-history of *Henry V* to express the *triumph* of resolution, a quality he evidently admires intensely. His film endures as a splendid pageant in celebration of singleness of purpose.

summary critique

As Peter Morris has noticed, *"Henry V* was the first Shakespeare film to gain not only critical acclaim but a wide measure of public support as well. In fact, it was a number of other firsts—the first Shakespeare film in color; the first to achieve a film style amenable to film presentations of Shakespeare and the first film to treat the soliloquy as thought, heard on the sound track, but not visibly spoken—a device which has been constantly adopted by other film directors. . . . However, the film did not find unanimous acceptance. It was criticized for some of its textual deletions which critics [such as James E. Phillips] claimed had oversimplified the character of King Henry; that Henry had been transformed from a complex and archaic symbol of ideal kingship into the dynamically appealing military leader he is in the film. Others [such as James Agate, and, recently, George W. Linden] felt that the progress from the Globe Theatre to the actualities of the Agincourt campaign and back again was a confusion of conventions."

In general, the film was more favorably received by film critics than theatre critics. However, there were some notable exceptions. Manny Farber, for example, while acknowledging that the film was "exciting, sometimes more so than the Shakespeare play," claimed that "the greatest letdown comes from the realization that so much of it is like what you find in boys' books, the *American Boy,* Disney movies, the action stories on boxes of Wheaties. . . . *Henry V* always looks a bit contrived (stagy and toylike), boyish, and heavy with décor and costuming the way a grade-school operetta is." On the other hand, theatre critic John Gassner asserted: "It is impossible to overpraise this cinematic transcription of the famous chronicle play; impossible to over-rate it as either Shakespeare or film."

Many of the most conflicting reactions are to be found in comments on the film's sets and the Globe Theatre scenes. High praise of the décor and costumes, from such critics as James Agee and Bosley Crowther, is balanced by adverse impressions from Manny Farber and George W. Linden. Siegfried Kracauer considered the opening sequence a "credit to Olivier's film sense," and even James Agate, whose response to the rest of the picture was only lukewarm, referred to the Globe scenes as "enchanting." On the other hand, Philip T. Hartung wrote off the opening sequence as "a great bore."

As far as characterization is concerned, critical disapproval appears to have concentrated on the comic personages. Thus, Philip Hartung found the scenes "showing Shakespeare's so-called clowns in action" as dull as he found the Globe sequences. Even Bosley Crowther, who considered much of the film "truly magnificent," objected that "Olivier has leaned perhaps too heavily toward the comic characters in the play. . . . And certainly the writing-in completely of the Falstaff deathbed scene . . . is obviously non-essential and just a bit grotesque."

Other adverse comment focused on the film's overt propaganda qualities. Thus Elliott Norton, while admiring the "magnificent success" of *Henry V* as an adaptation of Shakespeare, remarked that the "voice is the voice of Shakespeare, but the hand is sometimes the hand of Brendan Bracken, who was England's minister of information when the picture was made." Similarly, Hartung noticed, "Anti-Britishers may have some cause to complain that the English are again praising themselves and shooting their tops off about their own wares." However, in mitigation, he reminded anglophobes that "Henry is leading the British and expects no one else to do their fighting. . . . Furthermore, Americans, under similar circumstances, might well be proud of an American play written about an American leader who was as great, pious and noble as this English King. And, furthermore," he adds, "let us remember that it took the English to make this movie, the first Shakespeare-into-film that is real Shakespeare."

More recently than either Norton or Hartung, Raymond Durgnat, while actually accepting the film's "rousing jingoism" as one of its *raisons d'être,* has objected to the obscurity of some of the parallels to contemporary events. Thus, commenting on Henry's marriage to Katharine, he observes that "whether France here = France our ally, to whom Churchill had in 1940 impulsively proposed 'marriage,' or Germany our enemy whom we mustn't hate for ever, is quite ambiguous." (*A Mirror for England,* p. 109.)

In the most memorable lines ever written on *Henry V*, James Agee, who wrote about Olivier's film more perceptively and rapturously than any other critic, responded positively even to the propaganda: "I am not a Tory, a monarchist, a Catholic, a medievalist, an Englishman, or, despite all the good that it engenders, a lover of war: but the beauty and power of this traditional exercise was such that, watching it, I wished I was, thought I was, and was proud of it. I was persuaded, and in part still am, that every time and place has since been in decline, save one, in which one Englishman used language better than anyone has before or since, or ever shall; and that nearly the best that our time can say for itself is that some of us are still capable of paying homage to the fact."

films directed
by Laurence Olivier
bibliography
rental source

films directed
by Laurence Olivier

Henry V, 1944.

Hamlet, 1947–48. Starred Olivier in the title role; Jean Simmons as Ophelia; Basil Sydney as King Claudius; and Eileen Herlie as Queen Gertrude. The music was by William Walton.

Richard III, 1955. Starred Olivier as Richard III; Ralph Richardson as Buckingham; John Gielgud as Clarence; Cedric Hardwicke as Edward IV; Claire Bloom as Lady Anne. The music was by Walton.

The Prince and the Showgirl, 1956. Based on Terence Rattigan's play, *The Sleeping Prince*. Starred Olivier as The Regent; Marilyn Monroe as Elsie; Sybil Thorndike as the Queen Dowager.

Three Sisters, 1970.

bibliography

I. BOOKS AND ARTICLES DEALING GENERALLY WITH OLIVIER

Barker, Felix. *The Oliviers*. Philadelphia and New York: J. B. Lippincott Company, 1953.
Source of much basic information on *Henry V*.

Burton, Hal [ed.] *Great Acting*. New York: Hill and Wang, 1967.
Contains Kenneth Tynan's interview with Olivier.

Clark, Lee W. *Sir Laurence Olivier*. Unpublished dissertation offered in fulfillment of the M.S. degree at the Catholic University of America, Washington, D.C., 1967. Contains a bibliography. On file in New York Public Library Theater Collection, Lincoln Center. The section on *Henry V* is heavily indebted to Felix Barker's book.

Darlington, W. A. *Great Contemporaries: Laurence Olivier*. London, International Profiles, 1968.
Brief but lively survey of Olivier's career.

Dent, Alan. *Vivien Leigh: A Bouquet.* London: Hamish Hamilton, 1969.
Appreciation of the first Lady Olivier; peripheral relevance to study of Olivier.

Fairweather, Virginia. *Cry God for Larry: An intimate memoir of Sir Laurence Olivier.* London: Calder and Boyars, 1969.
Gossipy account that emphasizes Olivier's stage career since the 1950s.

Gelman, M. "Sir Laurence Olivier," *The Theatre* (New York), 2:2 (February 1960), 17, 44–45.

Lunari, Gigi. *Laurence Olivier.* Bologna; L. Capelli, 1959. Brief study of Olivier's career. In Italian.

Spiel, Hilde. *Sir Laurence Olivier.* Berlin, Rembrandt-Verlag, 1958. Slight essay on Olivier's career. In German.

Whitehead, Peter. *Olivier—Shakespeare.* London, Lorrimer Films Ltd., 1966. Brief text, in English, French and German. Profusely illustrated. Contains Olivier filmography—including screen roles—through *Khartoum* (1966).

II. SCREENPLAY AND TEXTS OF SHAKESPEARE'S HENRY V

Garrett, George P., et al., eds. *Film Scripts One.* New York: Appleton-Century-Crofts, 1971.
Contains the screenplay of Olivier's movie.

Shakespeare, William. *Henry V* edited by Alfred Harbage. Baltimore: Penguin Books, 1966.
Text to which all specific act, scene and line references are made in this study of the film.

Shakespeare, William. *Henry V with an Introduction* [by Max J. Herzberg] *and Additional Notes on the Laurence Olivier Film Production.* Pickering, Ontario: Global Publishing, 1947.
An edition of the play, evidently for high school students. Brief notes and questions on the play and the film; a short excerpt from the screenplay; some illustrations, mainly black and white.

III. BOOKS, ARTICLES AND REVIEWS PERTAINING TO OLIVIER'S HENRY V

Agate, James. Review. *The Times* (London), December 3, 1944.

Agee, James. Review. *Time,* April 8, 1946, 56–60.
"The movies have produced one of their rare great works of art."

———. Review. *The Nation,* July 20, 1946.
"It is not . . . the most exciting or inspiring or original film I have seen. But I cannot think of any that seems to be more beautiful . . . or more thoroughly satisfying."

———. Review. *The Nation,* August 3, 1946.
"Mr. Olivier and his associates . . . have done somewhere near all that talent, cultivation, taste, knowledgability, love of one's work—every excellence, in fact, short of genius—can be expected to do. . . ."

Alpert, Hollis. *The Dreams and the Dreamers.* New York: Macmillan, 1962, 241.
"I have found Laurence Olivier's *Henry V* far more satisfying on the screen than on stage, and for good reason. Shakespeare not only remained in the film, but was lifted into beautiful life."

Anonymous articles and reviews:

Review. *Cue,* June 15, 1946, 12–14.

Review. *Good Housekeeping,* 123 (July 1946), 15.

Review. *Life* 20 (May 20, 1946), 38–42. Mainly illustrations.

"Shakespeare's London in Technicolor." *New York Herald Tribune,* April 14, 1946, 3. Interesting details of the model of London built for the film.

"Olivier found England at war no place to film battle of 1415." *New York Herald Tribune,* June 2, 1946, 3.

"What Shakespeare dreamed Olivier attempts to provide through the films," *New York Sun* amusements section, April 16, 1946. Mainly illustrations.

Review. *Newsweek,* June 17, 1946, 102.

Review. *P.M. New York,* January 16, 1946, 9–11.

Review. *Scholastic* 49 (September 16, 1946), 40.

Review. *Variety,* April 24, 1946, 8.
". . . it will go right over the average audience."

"Recreates Medieval Paintings," *Vogue* 108 (September 1, 1946), 218–219.

Anstey, Edgar. Review. *The Spectator* (London), December 1, 1944, 502–503.

Aristarco, Guido. "Film di questi giorni: Enrico V," *Cinema*, n.s. 33, February 28, 1950.

B., G. "The film of *Henry V*," *English V* (1945), 107–108.

Bab, Julius. Review. *New Yorker Staats-Zeitung*, July 9, 1946. In German.

Balcon, Michael et al. *Twenty Years of British Film*. London: The Falcon Press, 1947. Contains Roger Manvell's essay on "The British Feature Film from 1940 to 1945," which includes on page 94 the comment: "*Henry V* . . . was a magnificent achievement with many sequences which made cinema of Shakespeare. . . . For the most part, however, this film could not make full use of the resources of the cinema since it was bound to the verbal wheel of Shakespeare's text written for a rhetorical theatre. The camera therefore had to record rather than take charge. . . ."

Bonfante, Egidio, "Enrico V," *Sequenze* I.i, September 1945.

Brown, John Mason. "Seeing Things: The Old Vic and *Henry V*," *The Saturday Review of Literature*, May 25, 1946, 27–28.

Chiarini, Luigi. "Cattivi Pensieri," *Cinema*, n.s., 33, February 28, 1950.

Clayton Hutton: see Hutton.

Crowther, Bosley. Review. *The New York Times*, June 18, 1946, 30.

"Olivier and his editor, Reginald Beck . . . have mounted the play with faithful service to the spirit and word. That service is as truly magnificent as any ever given to a Shakespearean script, both in visual conception and in the acting of an excellent cast."

————. "The Public and *Henry V*," *The New York Times*, June 23, 1946, 2:1.

————. "Classics Revisited," *The New York Times*, March 2, 1958, 2:1.

"It is perhaps the all-time supreme achievement of getting Shakespeare upon the screen."

Durgnat, Raymond. *A Mirror for England: British Movies from Austerity to Affluence*. London: Faber & Faber, 1970, 109–111.

The "*raisons d'être* [of Olivier's *Henry V*] are the prestige of

Shakespeare, a big battle, a rousing jingoism, and a shaky parallel to contemporary events. . . . For the film isn't about the historical Henry V, or even about Shakespeare's idea of Henry V. It's about *The Demi-Paradise,* Britain as happy home of poets and warrior alike. It remains interesting as a series of visual and verbal set pieces."

Eckert, Charles W., ed. *Focus on Shakespearean Films.* Englewood Cliffs, N.J.: Prentice-Hall, 1972. Useful anthology that includes Ian Johnson's essay "Merely Players," and reviews of *Henry V* by James Agee and Bosley Crowther. The filmography provides a detailed listing of Shakespeare films, arranged play by play.

Farber, Manny. Review. *The New Republic,* 115 (July 8, 1946), 14.
"Olivier's real feat . . . is in having directed a film that is always as exciting, sometimes more so, than the Shakespeare play."

Gassner, John. Review. *Forum* (Philadelphia) 10 (July 1946), 7–9.
"It is impossible to overpraise this cinematic transcription of the famous chronicle play; impossible to over-rate it as either Shakespeare or film. . . . It is sheer delight for two and a quarter hours."

Griffith, Richard. "The Film Since Then," in Paul Rotha's *The Film Till Now.* London: Spring Books, 1967, 553, 560.
"*Henry V* (1944) was probably the first instance of a legitimately photographed play, inasmuch as its structure was designed constantly to remind the spectator of the fact that it was a play and not a film."

Hartung, Philip T. Review. *The Commonweal,* June 21, 1946, 238–239.
"Technically, except for its static opening, it is an excellent job."

Hutton, C. Clayton. *The Making of Henry V.* London: Ernest J. Day, 1945. 72 pages. Illustrated in color and with drawings of the actors and producer, maps and other illustrations. Source of much factual information about the film.

Isaacs, Hermine R. Review. *Theatre Arts* 30 (April 1946), 217.

Johnson, Ian. "Merely Players," *Film and Filming,* April 1964, 41–

48. (Reprinted in Charles W. Eckert's *Focus on Shakespearean Films*.) An important essay, surveying many film adaptations of Shakespeare. On *Henry V* Johnson remarks: "It was one of the best creations of one of the brightest periods of British film-making, and has the qualities and style which typified that period: solidarity without staginess, a feeling of enthusiasm and a sweep, a great surge of confidence."

Kracauer, Siegfried. *Theory of Film.* New York: Oxford University Press, 1971, 227, 260.

"The battle in *Henry V* . . . is just a decorative pageant . . . the opening scenes . . . [do] credit to Olivier's film sense. It is an attempt to put the theatrical spectacle in brackets and offset the effect of its stylizations by a touch of camera reality."

Lejeune, C. A. Review. *The Observer* (London), November 26, 1944.

"What . . . Olivier has splendidly caught . . . is a salute to high adventure, a kind of boyish exaltation of man's grim work."

————. "London Steps Out: Premiere of *Henry V* rated as a Social Event," *The Observer* (London), December 31, 1944.

Lillich, Meredith. "Shakespeare on the Screen," *Films in Review,* June–July, 1956, 251–260.

"As cinema, *Henry V* was an unqualified work of art. As Shakespeare it may have far-reaching results."

Linden, George W. *Reflections on the Screen.* Belmont, California: Wadsworth Publishing Company, 1970, 21–22, 33.

"*Henry V* is no doubt the best adaptation of Shakespeare's various plays to appear on the screen; yet even it had disconcerting elements. The beginning reconstruction of the excitement and presence of the Globe Theatre is very compelling. We are then asked to move in imagination to the plains of Agincourt; but Shakespeare's language, as beautiful as it is, is simply irrelevant at this point."

Lindgren, Ernest. *The Art of the Film.* New York: Macmillan, 1968, 92.

"Sir Laurence Olivier's *Henry V* was a very fine filmed version of the play, but the magnificence of Shakespeare's verse alone, although spoken by our greatest actors, is not enough to make a great *film* in the true sense of the word . . . what is required is poetry *of* the film, instead of poetry *in* the film."

MacGowan, Kenneth. Review. *Hollywood Quarterly* 2 (October 1946), 92–94.

Manvell, Roger. "*Henry V* on the Films," *Britain Today,* March 1945, 25–26.

————. "Shakespeare as a Scriptwriter," *World Review,* May 1952, 56–59.

"Of Sir Laurence's productions, *Henry V* is more immediately effective than *Hamlet* because Shakespeare intended it to be visual—a pageant of history surrounding the robust figure of Henry, a character of the kind Olivier himself is so well fitted to portray."

———— and John Huntley. *The Technique of Film Music.* London and New York: Focal Press, 1957. Contains (pp. 80–91) an analysis of the music for the Agincourt sequence, and (pp. 78–79) a statement by William Walton on composing music for Olivier's Shakespeare films.

————. *Shakespeare and the Film.* New York: Praeger, 1971. Chapter 4 deals with "Laurence Olivier and the Filming of Shakespeare." The book has a useful bibliography.

McCarten, John. Review. *The New Yorker,* June 22, 1946, 40–42. "There is no air of pedantry about the film. . . . The freshness of *Henry V* is hugely enhanced by sets that do not depend for their effectiveness on humdrum realism. Foregrounds that look as tangible as the earth under your feet blend into backgrounds that might well be used to illustrate a fairy tale. . . . On the strength of *Henry V* . . . [Olivier] has emerged as the most imaginative film-maker around."

Merton, James. "Shakespeare Comes to the Films," *Christian Science Monitor,* March 30, 1946, 7.

"The production is truly Shakespearean. It follows the original text more closely than any of the many stage productions."

Morris, Peter. *Shakespeare on Film: An Index to William Shakespeare's Plays on Film.* Canadian Film Institute, Ottawa, 1964; 14 pages; 3–4, 8, deal with *Henry V.*

"If nothing else, *Henry V* proved the immense possibilities of film to remove Shakespeare from the top of the ivory towers and bring him back to the public. . . ."

Mosdell, D. Review. *Canadian Forum,* 26 (October 1946), 161.

Nathan, G. J. Review. *New York Journal-American,* June 17, 1946.

"The picture . . . is at least a fair approximation to the dramatic stage. . . . But with all its virtues I'll still take the theatre."

Norton, Elliott. "Drama and Politics mingled expertly in film *Henry V,*" *Boston Post,* April 7, 1946.

"I have rarely ever seen Shakespeare done with such magnificent success or British propaganda presented with such pushing insistence."

————. *"Henry V* Still the Best Screen Shakespeare," *Boston Daily Record,* March 24, 1958.

"Except for . . . *Henry V* . . . there has never been a really first rate movie production of a play by Shakespeare."

Ocampo, Victoria. *Henry V y Laurence Olivier, con los principales pasajes de la obra.* (Trans. Ricardo Baeza), Buenos Aires: Sur, 1947, 67 pages.

Ojetti, Paola. "Shakespeare sullo schermo," *Bianco e Nero* 9:5, July 1948.

Olivier, Laurence, "The Filming of *Henry V,*" in souvenir program: *G. C. F. Presents Laurence Olivier's Henry V by William Shakespeare* [1946].

Pandolfi, Vito. "L'Enrico V di Laurence Olivier," *La Rassegna d'Italia,* 3 (August 1948), 887–891.

Phillips, James E. "Adapted from a Play by W. Shakespeare," *Hollywood Quarterly* 2 (October 1946), 82–87.

"Among the remarkable achievements of Laurence Olivier's production of *Henry V* is the success with which an appealing and even exciting show is made out of material not generally regarded as the most promising that Shakespeare wrote. . . . Olivier has given us . . . a twentieth-century conception of a sixteenth-century conception of a historical fifteenth-century king."

Powell, Dilys. Review. *The Times* (London), November 26, 1944.

". . . this is a production finely felt and finely played. . . ."

Sammis, F. R. Review. *Photoplay,* 29 (November 1946), 1935.

Schwartz, Daniel. "The Present and Future of Shakespeare," *The New York Times Magazine,* May 12, 1946, 58.
Quotes Olivier's theories of filming.

Whitebait, William. Review. *The New Statesman and Nation,* December 2, 1944, 368.

Wyatt, E. V. R. "The Film of Henry V," *Catholic World* 163 (August 1946), 457–458.

IV. PUBLISHED MUSIC FROM HENRY V

Walton, William. *Two Pieces for Strings, from the Film Music Henry V.* London, Oxford University Press, 1947, 4 pages. Contains: "Passacaglia: Death of Falstaff," and "Touch her soft lips and part."

————. *Suite from Henry V.* London, Oxford University Press, Music Department, 1964. Miniature score. "Composed in 1943 for the film . . . and . . . adapted for concert use by Muir Mathieson, with the composer's authorization." Contains: "Overture: The Globe Playhouse," "Passacaglia: Death of Falstaff," "Touch her soft lips and part," and "Agincourt Song."

V. PHOTOGRAPH RECORDINGS (undated)

Henry V Collected Excerpts. Laurence Olivier and the Philharmonia Orchestra conducted by William Walton. HMV C3583/6. 4 disks (78 rpm).

Henry V Excerpts. Laurence Olivier with Philharmonia Orchestra and Chorus conducted by Walton. Victor M-1128. 4 disks (78 rpm).

Henry V Film Music, 1945. Excerpts. Philharmonia Orchestra. Victor LM 1926 (78 rpm).

Henry V: Two Pieces for Strings. Contains: "Death of Falstaff," and "Touch her soft lips and part." Philharmonia Orchestra conducted by Walton. HMV C3480 (78 rpm).

Olivier: In Scenes from Hamlet and Henry V. Excerpts from Act III sc.1, Prologue to Act IV, Act IV sc.1, Act IV sc.3, The battle of Agincourt, Burgundy's speech, Epilogue. The Philharmonia Orchestra conducted by Walton. RCA Victor LM 1924 (33 rpm).

Sir William Walton: Music from Shakespeare Films: Original Scores from Sir Laurence Olivier's *Richard III, Hamlet, Henry V. Henry V* music includes: "Overture: The Globe Playhouse," "Passacaglia: Death of Falstaff," "Charge and Battle," "Touch her soft lips and part," and "Agincourt Song." Jacket notes by Muir Mathieson. Angel 36198 (33 rpm); Seraphim S-60205.

Filmharmonic 70: Highlights from a Festival of Film Music. Includes "Battle of Agincourt: from *Henry V*" and "St. Crispin's Day" spoken by James Mason. The Royal Philharmonic Orchestra conducted by Muir Mathieson. Polydor Standard recording 2682 #020. (33 rpm.) Two disks; the *Henry V* pieces are on record two.

VI. "LES TRÈS RICHES HEURES"

Limbourg, Pol de. "Les Tres Riches Heures du Duc de Berry," [Calendar by Pol de Limbourg and Jean Colombe; text by Henri Malo], *Verve* 2:7 (April–July 1940). Contains twelve characteristic pages of the calendar in full color. It was probably these reproductions that Olivier brought to the attention of his art director.

rental source

A 16 mm. Technicolor print of *Henry V* may be rented from Walter Reade 16, 241 East 34th Street, New York, N.Y. 10016. Telephone 212-683-6300.